# THE FATAL CUP

THOMAS GRIFFITHS WAINEWRIGHT AND THE
STRANGE DEATHS OF HIS RELATIONS

John Price Williams

**The Fatal Cup** © 2018 John Price Williams & Markosia Enterprises, Ltd. All Rights Reserved. Reproduction of any part of this work by any means without the written permission of the publisher is expressly forbidden. Published by Markosia Enterprises, PO BOX 3477, Barnet, Hertfordshire, EN5 9HN. FIRST PRINTING, March 2018. Harry Markos, Director.

*Paperback:* ISBN 978-1-911243-70-0
*Hardback:* ISBN 978-1-911243-69-4
*eBook:* ISBN 978-1-911243-71-7

*Book design by: Ian Sharman*

FRONT COVER PICTURE:
*Wainewright's ironic self-portrait, drawn in crayon on the back of a medical form while he was working at the hospital in Hobart. It is the only likeness of him known to exist. This and other Wainewright portraits in the book appear by kind permission of the Nuttall family.*

www.markosia.com

First Edition

## PROLOGUE

*Van Diemen's Land, November 1837*
Slowly and carefully the weathered barque *Susan* nudged her way up the dangerous strait between the South East Cape and Tasman Head.

Even more cautiously she passed the underwater rock that had ripped the bottom out of another ship *George III* two years before, leading to the loss of 120 lives.

Up she came though the d'Entrecasteaux Channel, up the Derwent River until the pilot brought her finally into Sullivan's Cove.

As the anchor of the *Susan* rattled down, a red flag was hoisted on the shore. It meant "Convicts from England".

It had been a relatively quick passage for a convict ship – 109 days after clearing the Isle of Wight to sail to the other end of the world, to Hobartown, Van Diemen's Land, later to be renamed Tasmania.

The first part had been easy, with light winds and agreeable time spent on the open deck, but after rounding the Cape into the Roaring Forties, there had been a month of westerly gales and raging seas, according to the account of one who sailed in her.

Hatches had been battened down for weeks on end, and the noisome prison deck below was frequently flooded, and the water swilled to and fro as the *Susan* pitched and rolled violently night and day.

Cooped up in this sodden, filthy world were nearly

300 men, another cargo of criminality exported from England to be dumped out of sight and mind in "this dust-hole of Empire", as Colonial Secretary, Lord Stanley called it. An island penal colony the British did not even want, but had occupied only to prevent the French acquiring it.

Among those below, crippled by the fever of rheumatism, lay Convict 2325 Thomas Griffiths Wainewright. Age: 43. Occupation: there were many; dandy, painter, essayist. Swindler. Murderer?

How had it come to this? The perfumed and jewelled exquisite who affected a quizzing glass and lemon yellow gloves in the literary and artistic salons of fashionable London reduced to wretchedness and a sentence of Transportation to Parts beyond the Seas.

The essayists Charles Lamb and William Hazlitt and the poet John Clare had been his friends and he had contributed to London's leading literary magazine. The lions of literary and artistic London came to dine with the elegant Wainewright at his lavish London apartment and the fine country house at Turnham Green in Chiswick.

Had he not been praised as an artist by William Blake, exhibited at the Royal Academy in London, had claimed the academy's President, the famous portraitist Sir Thomas Lawrence, as a childhood friend, and the academy's Keeper, Henry Fuseli, the Gothic fantasist as "the god of his worship"?

Had he not followed Fuseli's lead-lined coffin to St Paul's in the funeral procession? Did the crowds not marvel as they saw the dandy as he rode in an open coach behind a hearse which was drawn by six black horses, accompanied by pages bearing funeral feathers, four porters on foot in black silk dresses and eight pages bearing truncheons?

There were other coffins he was to follow after Fuseli's – in humbler and much stranger circumstances; those of his uncle, George Griffiths, his mother-in-law and finally his sister-in-law, Helen Phoebe Frances Abercromby.

The three had died in agony. The deaths of all of them had benefited him. He and his wife Eliza had tried, and failed, to defraud eight London insurance companies to pay off enormous debts.

But what had finally brought him to judgement was an audacious swindle on the Bank of England, for which he had narrowly escaped the hangman and was now leading to a lifetime of exile in this land he was later to call a "moral sepulchre".

His story is one of reckless spending, of talent squandered, of privilege abused and of greed unsated.

But was he the killer that everyone has made him out to be?

# CHAPTER 1

# THE MAKING OF THE DANDY

Thomas Griffiths Wainewright has been damned as a murderer from that day to this. After his transportation those who had been his friends and acquaintances were quick to pass judgement. They queued up to castigate him. John Forster, the critic and biographer of Dickens called him an "unscrupulous and unsparing murderer".

His sister-in-law, Helen, had died of poisoning after she had swallowed from what the Attorney-general was to call a "fatal cup" and Wainewright was accused of saying that he had killed her "because her ankles were too thick". He was said to wear among his many rings one with a secret compartment that contained the deadly poison strychnine. Victorian authors fell on the case with relish to produce spine-chillers.

Oscar Wilde was fascinated by him, describing him as "not merely a poet and a painter, an art critic, an antiquarian, and a writer of prose, an amateur of beautiful things and a dilettante of things delightful, but also a forger... and a subtle and secret poisoner almost without rival in this or any other age".[1]

As recently as the year 2000, the UK poet laureate, Andrew Motion produced what he called

---

[1] *Wilde. O. Pen Pencil and Poison.* Fortnightly Review. 1889

a "confection", a fictional confession, purported to have been written by Wainewright in his dying days in Van Diemen's Land. It was accompanied by copious notes and called *Wainewright the Poisoner*.[2]

But there is no proof that Wainewright administered poison to anyone. There were suspicious deaths among those close to him and one of them at least was murder in which he was probably complicit. So who was responsible?

New research into documents not seen for nearly two centuries has cast a different light upon his extraordinary life and on the deaths of his relations. And for the first time it can be disclosed what happened to the real killer.

It is time to look at the evidence again.

Thomas Griffiths Wainewright was born into privilege in Linden House, a mansion bought by books, which lay off the Great West Road in the pleasant little village of Turnham Green, five miles south west of the centre of London, notable for one of the largest battles in the English Civil War in November 1642 when the Parliamentarians blocked King Charles' advance on London. Linden House

---

[2.] *Motion, A. Wainewright the Poisoner*, Faber, 2000. After its publication a retired antiquarian bookseller, Marc Vaulbert de Chantilly, pointed out to Motion that it contained 250 factual errors. de Chantilly then produced a booklet castigating Motion's methods and detailing every error. *Wainewright the Poisoner: an example of Andrew Motion's "high scholarship"*. The Vanity Press of Bethnal Green, 2000. In the *Guardian* of 26 Feb. 2000, Motion congratulated de Chantilly on "like all biographers and scholars, adding to an existing store of knowledge."

The imposing front of Linden House, Wainewright's childhood home in Turnham Green, London, to which he was to return after his grandfather's death and in which his uncle George and his mother-in-law were to die suddenly.

*Chiswick Public Libraries*

stood in more than three acres of well-timbered ground, and was noted for its limes and for the lindens from which it took its name.[3]

The balustraded wall around the nine-bedroomed house cut off the noise of hooves and jingling reins from the busy High Road in the parish of Chiswick and its occupants strolled over trim lawns and neat gravel paths

It had a 300-foot frontage, a huge library, greenhouses, coach houses, stabling for seven horses, a kitchen garden and a very large lawn and

---

[3.] Linden House was demolished in 1879. A street of houses called Linden Gardens now stands on the site.

paddock, according to an auctioneer's catalogue in 1832. It was a 'capital house', commented one observer admiringly.

To the imposing portico and the great door set in the encompassing walls came the cream of London's literary society, for this was the home of Dr. Ralph Griffiths, bookseller, publisher and editor of the *Monthly Review*, which he had founded in 1749, the most influential literary journal of its kind in Georgian London,

Its only rival, the *Critical Review*, run by Tobias Smollett, denounced it as being conducted "by a parcel of obscure hirelings under the restraint of a bookseller and his wife, who presume to revise, alter and amend the articles occasionally."

Dr. Griffiths was the grandfather of Thomas Griffiths Wainewright – to whom he gave his middle name – and a formative influence on his infant life. Griffiths himself was a Shropshire village lad, who had started life as a watchmaker's apprentice at Stone in Staffordshire, then pulled himself up by ambition and hard dealing to become a bookseller in the capital.

He was a hard master to those "obscure hirelings" who ran his magazine for him. The splendours of Linden House were paid for partly by the toil of his contributors. One of the poorly-paid hacks who managed to break free was a schoolmaster named Oliver Goldsmith, later to become famous as the author of *The Vicar of Wakefield* and *She Stoops to Conquer*. After five months as a sub-editor and 12 contributions he left disillusioned. Mrs Griffiths, who took a hand in running the magazine with her husband, accused him of unpunctuality and idleness; Goldsmith retorted that she had rationed what he ate and cut what he wrote.

Like many such magazines, the privilege of appearing in it was thought sufficient not to merit any great payment for the labours involved.

In its heyday the magazine was earning £2,000 a year, a huge sum in those days, and more than £150,000 in today's money.[4] The good Doctor Griffiths – his degree was honorary from the University of Philadelphia – was a very rich man and starved his contributors to feast his friends.

As he entertained in his mansion or whirled the few miles to London in one of his two carriages he could reflect with satisfaction on the good fortune he had striven so hard to earn. The *Dictionary of National Biography* described him as "lively, free-hearted and intelligent." He was also snobbish, arrogant and extravagant; failings which he passed on in good measure to his grandson.

As well as the magazine there was another goldmine. He had bought for 20 guineas a manuscript by a former British Consul in Smyrna; his name was John Cleland, the title of the work *Fanny Hill or The Memoirs of a Woman of Pleasure*. Dr. Griffiths published – and the erotic book was a

---

[4.] The 19th Century equivalent of sums of money to today's values throughout this book are taken from the Bank of England's online Inflation Calculator for 2017. As the Bank points out, the figures should be taken with caution as the definitions of goods and services included in the price index have changed. For example, a family's food and clothes today are very different to those of a typical family 200 years ago.

The rear of Linden House shortly before it was demolished in 1878 to make way for terraces of Victorian houses in what is now called Linden Gardens.

*Chiswick Public Libraries*

runaway success; he was said to have made more than £20,000 from it.

The unfortunate Cleland received only his pittance and a reprimand from the Privy Council. Another bookseller who wrote in more titillating details was put in the pillory.

Griffiths even puffed the book in his own magazine – without disclosing his interest. "The style has peculiar neatness and the characters are naturally drawn." He didn't specify to what, and added disingenuously: "as to the step recently taken to suppress this book we are really at a loss to account for it."

His opinion was much the same as that expressed by defence witnesses at Bow Street Court in London more than 200 years later, when the Magistrate ordered 171 paperback copies to be forfeited under the Obscene Publications Act.

By his second wife, Griffiths had two daughters; the first died as a child, the second in childbirth. This was Ann, pretty and highly-intelligent who had married at the age of 19, Thomas Wainewright of Sloane Street, Chelsea. The marriage is recorded in the registers of Chiswick Parish Church:

> *Thomas Wainewright, Esquire, of the Parish of St. Luke, Chelsea, in the County of Middlesex, Bachelor, and Ann Griffiths, of the Parish of Chiswick in the same County, Spinster, a Minor, by and with the lawful consent of Ralph Griffiths, Esquire, the natural and lawful father of the said Minor, were married by licence this 13th day of December 1792, by me, James Trebeck A.M., Vicar.*

The young couple lived at Chiswick, probably at Linden House with Dr. Griffiths; the mansion was big enough for them all. But he had not approved of the marriage, according to the *Dictionary of National Biography*, despite giving his consent. Then tragedy; on October 11, 1794, after being married for fewer than two years, Ann died giving birth to a son. Dr Griffiths, who was by then 74, had lost a daughter and gained a grandson on the same day.

He was christened Thomas after his father and Griffiths after his grandfather; his mother Ann was the first of many people close to him who were to die suddenly.

The *Gentleman's Magazine* noted her death in its *Obituary of Notable Persons*:

> *She is greatly regretted on account of her amiable disposition and uncommon accomplishments. She is supposed to have understood the writings of Mr. Locke as well as, perhaps, any person of either sex now living.*

Uncommon indeed in Georgian England for a woman of 21 to be a recognised authority on the works of a philosopher, but being brought up at table with the cream of literary London she would have had a rare and unusual grasp of such matters and had her father's huge library at her disposal.

The baby was left to be brought up by his grandparents and his father – a lawyer, one of the 12 children of a prosperous solicitor of Hatton Garden. Like his wife, he too, died young, a few years later, leaving the young Thomas an orphan, but in the care of his wealthy but aged grandparents.

It was before he was nine, for in Dr. Griffiths' will, dated June 1803, the boy's father is referred to as "the late". It was a very strange will that Dr. Griffiths made in June that year, four months before his own death at the age of 83.

## IN THE PREROGATIVE COURT OF CANTERBURY

> *This is the last Will and Testament of me, Ralph Griffiths, of Turnham Green, in the*

County of Middlesex, Doctor of Laws. Whereas on the marriage of my late daughter, Ann Griffiths, with the late Thomas Wainewright Esquire, I advanced a certain sum of money and covenanted that after my death a further sum should be paid by my personal representatives as a marriage portion for my said daughter and whereas my grandson Thomas Wainewright is become entitled to such property so advanced by me to his mother my Will that neither he the said Thomas Wainewright nor his trustees for him shall demand any further sum out of my estate as I hereby declare that the sum already paid with that which is covenanted to be paid is all that I intend for my said grandson. And with regard to the rest and residue of my estate and effects of what kind of nature soever it is my Will and intention that the same should be divided according to the statute for the distributions between my wife and my son George Edward Griffiths, and that I should die intestate save and except as to what I have declared regarding my said grandson Thomas Wainewright.

In witness whereof I have hereunto set my hand and seal this seventh day of June in the year of Our Lord one thousand eight hundred and three."

This is unlikely, at his great age, to have been his first will. Why did he go to such lengths to ensure that his young grandson would get not a penny more than he had settled on his dead daughter and husband?

There is some evidence that the bluff doctor - described by John Forster, the biographer of

Dickens as "a mean-spirited tyrant" - had developed a dislike of the young orphan who roamed the corridors of Linden House. He is named in the will twice as Thomas Wainewright; his second Christian name – Griffiths – which came from his grandfather himself, is omitted. It seems almost as though the old man were trying to disown him. It would have irked him mightily if he had known that one day the lad would inherit the lot.

It has been suggested that the young Wainewright might already have been showing a childish cunning which turned his grandfather against him. But of this, of course, there is no proof.

The bequest that did come to the boy was £5,000 invested at the Bank of England in Navy five per cent annuities – his greed and reckless spending when he plundered the inheritance years later was to cause his downfall. The settlement was in the name of three trustees: his uncle, Robert Wainewright; Edward Smith Foss a relative on his mother's side, and Foss's, son, also Edward, whom Wainewright regarded as a cousin. Under the terms of the will, Wainewright could not touch the capital at any time; all he could draw on was the dividends of £250 a year (£23,500). What is more, the capital would never come to him. The trusteeship would continue for his descendants. But that annual income, guaranteed by the Bank of England was enough to keep him in some style - the wage of a labourer in England, with no guarantee of employment was not much more than £20 a year.

The restriction in the will was to set Wainewright on the road to crime. For what could be more galling for the debt-ridden profligate he was to become, than to have a considerable sum of money just out of reach – money which he regarded morally as being his own? The frustration and the temptation were to become so unbearable that he was willing to risk a death sentence by swindling the Bank of England and then to gain from mysterious deaths of his relatives.

With old Dr. Griffiths gone, Wainewright was brought up by his grandmother the shrewish, hard-headed business woman, who died in 1812, and her son George, an amiable easy-going bachelor and dabbler in the arts who took up the editorship of the *Monthly Review.*

George's delights were planting tropical trees and building new conservatories in the grounds of Linden House. By 1822 money seems to have become tight, as part of the land was sold off to the Duke of Devonshire for £800.

The young Wainewright had a lonely if privileged upbringing, with a firm grounding in the arts; his grandfather's dinner table and library had seen to that. Though he was to dismiss this in one of his essays years later:

> *As a boy I was placed frequently in literary society; a giddy, flighty disposition prevented me from receiving thence any advantage.*

This was not true, the advantages were considerable; he was brought up in a bookish hothouse and knew the famous authors of the day who came to dine. He acquired a considerable body of knowledge which was to prove most important as it later gave him an entrée into artistic society.

His formal education was completed at Dr. Charles Burney's newly-opened academy at Hammersmith, and probably at his other, more famous Academy at Greenwich. Dr. Burney was a distant relative, a contributor to the *Monthly Review,* an antiquarian and one of the great classical scholars of his time. It was here that Wainewright added to his Latin, Greek and the considerable body of knowledge which he delighted to display with such panache in his later essays.

Here, too, another talent burgeoned. He became proficient as a draughtsman. W. Carew Hazlitt, his first proper biographer, who collected and edited his essays in 1880, was able to see the book in which he drew at Dr. Burney's. "It displays great talent and natural feeling" he recorded. The book is now lost. Wainewright himself declared: "The little attention I gave to anything was directed to painting, or rather to an admiration of it." It was more than admiration; he decided to become an artist himself.

He was 19, articulate, well-schooled, well-connected and, most importantly, had a comfortable independent income.

But – and this was one of the roots of his tragedy – not enough to keep up the wardrobe and the inclinations of a dandy, for such he had become. His dandyism was to become more than a passing phase of youthful extravagance; it was the start of the profligacy which led to his downfall.

He had already studied painting under John Linnell, friend of Blake and an accomplished landscape and portrait artist, but to become anything of an artist himself it was necessary to become apprenticed to one of the successful, fashionable Royal Academicians. He chose Thomas Phillips, whose portraiture was already famous. The National Portrait Gallery in London calls him prolific, since he completed more than 700 portraits, many of them of the great men of the day in the arts and sciences... At Phillips' studios in George Street, off Hanover Square, the young dandy mixed the paints and met the famous. At that time Phillips was painting literary figures, a series commissioned by the publisher, John Murray.

To the George Street studio came Coleridge, Southey, Byron and others. Phillips' famous 1813 portrait of Byron in dramatic Albanian costume now hangs in the National Portrait Gallery in London; it is one of three versions that he produced. He also painted four versions of Byron in a plain blue cloak one of which was exhibited at the Royal Academy in 1814. At the same time that this was painted, Wainewright himself portrayed the poet – in a similar pose.

Byron may have remembered the young apprentice from his sittings, of which there were at least four. He is said to have told his great friend the peculiar Lady Blessington - who was said to have transformed herself from an Irish slattern to a lady of quality - of the first man he ever saw wearing pale-lemon coloured gloves, "and devilish well they looked." Many have attributed the wearing of these to Wainewright and he himself refers to wearing them in one of his essays. Gloves were a particular signifier of the dandy. The foppish Count d'Orsay, part of the scandalous *ménage à trois* with Lady Blessington and her husband, was

Wainewright's short apprenticeship to the fashionable portraitist Thomas Phillips brought him into contact with many of the literary and artistic figures of the day. When Phillips painted Byron, Wainewright did too and his painting still survives at Byron's ancestral home in Nottinghamshire.

*Newstead Abbey*

said to require six pairs of scented gloves to see him through the day.

Wainewright's 'Byron' was auctioned at Christies in 1892 and was bought for 19 guineas by one of the Colnaghi family, the print-sellers, whom Wainewright was to know so well at the height of his literary and artistic success. According to the National Portrait Gallery, the picture was offered to them in 1936 by Lady d'Erlanger, who was disposing of Byron memorabilia, but they refused it because it was a copy, not an original Phillips, so it went to Newstead Abbey, Byron's ancestral home, in Nottinghamshire, where it still hangs and is said to be one of the very few of Wainewright's works which survive in Britain.

There was another notable painting in oils from around 1816. It was of Edward Foss, not just his relative and a trustee of the bequest but a childhood friend. Foss would later be the one who sent Wainewright to his downfall.

Apprenticeship in George Street did not suit Wainewright, he had too high an opinion of his own talents. After a few restless months, he cast around for something else to do, something with more excitement than the discipline of learning a profession. He recorded years later: "ever to be whiled away by new and flashy gauds (*showy ornamental things*), I postponed the pencil to the sword". He was going to join the army.

# CHAPTER 2

# AN OFFICER AND GENTLEMAN

The "new and flashy gauds" were the yellow facings and silver lace of The 16th (the Bedfordshire) Regiment of Foot. It was probably the peacock finery of the young Guards and dragoon officers strutting around London which had attracted Wainewright to the Army. He was once reported as saying airily: "No artist should serve as a soldier unless he is permitted to design his own uniform."

He no doubt imagined himself as a dashing officer in a fashionable regiment, taking time off from the busy social round to perform feats of arms which could later be recounted at the dinner table. The truth was to be very different.

Coleridge had joined as a private, but Wainewright bought his way in as an officer, or rather, tolerant Uncle George Griffiths had to put up the money - £400 in cash demanded for the lowest rank of officer - as Wainewright had an allowance of only £250 a year.

It must have pained him that Uncle George was not more generous; £400 was the minimum price of a commission, and that in a county infantry regiment. The buying of commissions had gone on since the 17th century - the more you paid, the higher the prestige you enjoyed. It preserved the senior officer class as an exclusive cadre, built on wealth and social privilege, of which Wainewright had neither. He was on the bottom rung as an ensign; today's rank would be a second lieutenant. (The equivalent in a cavalry regiment was a cornet; both ranks were abolished in the army reforms of 1871, as was the purchase of commissions).

With £735 to spare he could have become a cornet in the dragoons (which, in fact, he later hinted he had been) and £1,050 would have bought a coveted cornetcy in the fashionable Horse Guards, according to the table of prices for commissions printed in the Army's General Regulations and Orders of 1815.

The recruiting agent in London for the 16th Foot was named Brett, his office was in Soho. It was there that Wainewright went with his £400, and his application to join the regiment is still in the National Archives[1] with a covering letter from Brett:

*Gerrard Street, Soho*          *11th April 1814*

*Sir,*
*I beg leave to enclose for the consideration of His Royal Highness the Commander-in-Chief the enclosed application from Mr T.G. Wainewright for the purchase of an Ensigncy with the 16th Regiment of Foot, and to add that the regulated purchase money has been lodged with me. I have the honour to be, Sir, your most obedient, humble servant.*
*P. Brett*

Wainewright wrote:

*Colonel Torren*

---

[1] WO 31/ 397

*I beg you will be pleased to obtain for me His Majesty's permission to purchase an Ensigncy in the 16th Foot.*

*In case his Majesty shall be graciously pleased to permit me to purchase the said Commission, I do declare and certify, upon the word and honour of an officer and a gentleman that I will not, either now or at any future time give by any means or in any shape whatever, directly, or indirectly, any more than the sum of £400 – being the price limited by His Majesty's Regulation as the full value of the said commission.*

*I have the honour to be your most obedient humble servant.*

*T.G. Wainewright*

*Officer commanding the 16th Regiment of Foot –*

*I hereby declare that I verily believe the established Regulation with regard to Price, is intended to be strictly complied with, and that no clandestine bargain subsists between the Parties concerned.*

*In the absence of Lieutenant General Sir George Prevost Bart*

*P. Brett*

The giving of his word as an "officer and gentleman" was the formality to prevent trafficking in commissions. So, having paid Brett his fee of £4 11s 2s, Wainewright became on April 14, 1814, an instant officer, the ninth ensign in the 16th Foot, replacing one Mahoney, who had been promoted.

The artistic, dilettante 20-year-old used to fluttering his way around London's literary salons was now banished to the cold and wet south of Ireland. The regiment had been based for the preceding few months, at Fermoy, a small town on the river Blackwater in County Cork and it had been recruiting hard as it was under-strength.

In its last overseas tour, in Surinam and Barbados, 27 officers and 500 men had died from yellow fever. And the misfortunes had continued. On the way home, the troopship *Islam*, with a battalion on board, had been wrecked on the Tuskar Rock, off the coast of Ireland, a notorious graveyard for ships. A history of the Regiment says that although only one man, one woman and "some children" were drowned; all the arms, luggage and appointments were lost. The survivors were saved by workmen building a lighthouse on the rock at the time; none too soon, it would seem.

As the new ensign was waiting to be gazetted, having his uniform made, and choosing his sword, the 16th left the barracks at Fermoy, and set sail from nearby Monkstown for Canada. The war with the United States was not two years old and the 16th was being posted to guard the Canadian border against the threat of attack from the south. Wainewright's first chance of military glory had vanished.

While the regiment was still at sea, he arrived at the huge barracks in Fermoy, the final part of which had been completed a few years previously.

It was the largest military base in the west of Ireland, with accommodation for more than 180 officers, 2,800 other ranks and 152 horses. But when Wainewright arrived there was only a vestige of his regiment left.

The monthly *Regimental Return*, dated May 25th 1814, four days before the regiment landed in Quebec, shows that the garrison in Fermoy was down to six officers and 60 men.

In command was Captain John Galloway, under him Lieutenants W.G. Hasleham, John O'Brien, Darby Mahoney and another ensign, John O'Donnell, who joined three weeks after Wainewright. They were all Irish, and the first three all regulars. The young dilettante must soon have tired of their provincialism, and of Fermoy itself, whose streets, according to a local account of the time, were "partially-paved".

Dreams of action were evaporating in the empty barracks in the wet south of Ireland. As the rest of the 16th was garrisoning Quebec and Montreal and setting up post at Chambly and Coteau du Lac, Ensign Wainewright was writing orderly and guard reports.

He was to accustom himself "to give his words of command not only with energy and precision but with that firm, confident manly voice..." according to the *Regimental Companion,* somewhat of a challenge for one who lisped and lacked the discipline to be either energetic or precise. He should also have been having a "frequent intercourse, not only with geographical charts and books upon mathematics, but likewise the application of their different principles to practical experiments." An arid prospect for one of Wainewright's artistic disposition.

Apart from entering into practical experiments with a notable lack of enthusiasm there was little for the officers to do except talk and drink. Wainewright wrote eight years later of his time at Fermoy: "the noisy audacity of military conversation, united to the fragrant fumes of whisky-punch (ten tumblers every evening without acid!)* obscured my recollection of Michel Angelo (sic) as in a dun fog". (It's not clear what he meant by acid; whisky punch is usually made by adding lemons and sugar).

But if the drink and the talk failed, Fermoy itself had a few distractions to offer. There was a circulating library, a newsroom and billiard room at the biggest hotel. "The necessities and luxuries of life are found here in as great profusion as in any of the larger towns in Ireland" declared Samuel Lewis's *Topographical Dictionary of Ireland.*

The highlight of the year came in September; a week's racing on a course north of the town which was also used for military exercises. Even with all these small distractions, life in an empty regimental depot was very dull, as the *Monthly Returns* show. Most months there were no orders from London or Dublin. When letters did arrive they usually dealt with minor matters, such as ammunition or provisioning.

Or perhaps Captain Galloway was so bemused by whisky punch that he forgot to enter in the *Returns* all that he should have done; a tart note from the Adjutant-General in Dublin that September directed him to "be particular in examining them."

The boredom of Ireland was soon to end. By January 1815 this rump of the regiment had moved to Hilsea barracks at Portsmouth and by the following month to nearby Tipnor, the magazine and gunpowder works. Wainewright was granted leave by the Commandant from February 11th, and should have returned by the 13th, but there was no sign of him.

By the 15th he was posted absent without leave, and ten days later Captain Galloway noted in his *Return*:[2] "It is presumed some accident must have happened to him, as there has been no account whatsoever from him." Captain Galloway was obviously taking a charitable view of the disappearance of his ensign.

But a month later Wainewright was still missing. The March *Return* pointed out that every effort had been made to trace him: "Ensign Wainewright was written to agreeable (sic) to the address he left, but no answer has been received; his friends were there written to, who stated they understood he was lying ill at Bath, but that as soon as certain information could be obtained I should be informed thereof."

By the time Captain Galloway wrote this Wainewright had been missing for six weeks, and without a word of explanation. However grievous his illness, it seems that he had been able to let his friends know, but not his regiment. Was the illness a precursor of the "acute disease" as he called it, which was to attack him within a few months? It seems more likely, and more in character, that he had become so bored and restless that the idea of returning after leave to a soulless military life miles from his London haunts had become intolerable.

Oscar Wilde was to write much later that the "reckless dissipated life of his companions failed to

---

[2] WO 17/291

satisfy the refined artistic temperament of one who was made for other things".

But return he did eventually, for by the end of April he was back on the strength. In the British army in the 19th century, absence without leave automatically became desertion after 21 days, for which the penalties were very severe. No record of Wainewright being disciplined has been discovered. Perhaps the rules were elastic in the languid world of the officer class.

For example, Lord Cardigan, he of the disastrous charge of the Light Brigade, had bought himself a colonelcy for £40,000 and in the first two years of his service in the 11th Hussars was with his regiment for only four weeks.[3]

During Wainewright's long absence, Napoleon had escaped from Elba and marched on Paris; another European conflict was imminent. Orders went out to the 16th in Canada to return home at once.

The regiment landed at Portsmouth in August, two months too late for Waterloo, though it eventually went on to join the army of occupation. But Wainewright took no part in all this; in May he resigned his commission. He may have been asked to do so after his long absence; more probably the thought of further service was unbearable. He had lasted barely a year, and that with a long absence in between.

His last few days in the Army he spent at Fort Cumberland, the bastioned stronghold at

---

[3.] Woodham-Smith, C. *The Reason Why*. Penguin, 1953

Portsmouth which commanded the approach to the marshes and Langstone Harbour.

As he looked across Spithead to the Isle of Wight he could not have imagined that the next time he would see it, 22 years' later, would be as a convict bound for the other side of the world. But there was no thought of ignominy now; on May 15th he sold his commission and his name appears for the last time in the Army List for June 1815. "Augustus Losack to be ensign by purchase *vice* Wainewright retd."

Another career had failed, and he later dismissed this failure characteristically in one of his essays: "Several apparently trifling chances determined me against this mode of killing Time and *humans*." The italics are his.

# CHAPTER 3

## "THE BRINK OF MERE INSANITY"

He was free; the restraints of communal life has been lifted, he was his own master again. He wrote:

*I was idle on the town, my blessed art touched her renegade; by her pure and high influences the noisome mists were purged; my feelings, parched hot and tarnished were renovated with a cool fresh bloom, childly, simple, beautiful to the simple-hearted.*

He found solace in Wordsworth, weeping, as he said, tears of happiness and gratitude over his poems. But this elevated state did not last, for he fell ill. His serene state was broken, he was to say in one of his essays...

*...like a vessel of clay by "acute disease, succeeded by a relaxation of the muscles and nerves which depressed me. Hypochondriasis! Ever shuddering on the brink of mere insanity!*

Oscar Wilde surmised that Wainewright had "wandered through that terrible valley of melancholia from which so many great, perhaps greater, spirits have never emerged".

The illness seems to have had a critical effect on his life and theories have been propounded to suggest that what could be recognised now as severe depression had turned him into a reckless spender and a criminal.

Havelock Ellis, the psychologist, who was also a literary critic and essayist, described Wainewright "the perfect picture of the instinctive criminal in his most highly-developed shape" and concluded in his book *The Criminal* in 1901 that he was probably insane at the time.

"It is extremely probable that he never recovered from the effects of that illness......if we possessed a full knowledge of every instinctive criminal we should always be able to put our hands on some organically-morbid spot".

Jonathan Curling, who published a biography of Wainewright in 1938, hazarded a guess at sleeping sickness, *Encephalitis lethargica*, which could lead to cerebral derangement and turn a man into a criminal.

In January 2017, I showed one of London's leading consultant psychiatrists, Dr Edward Burns, the above eight paragraphs to seek his medical opinion. He was told Wainewright was possibly a murderer, according to previous reports, but given no information about his past.

He dismissed Curling's hypothesis saying it was unlikely that a physical illness would turn him into a murderer. People often searched for reasons, such as an illness, which turned for someone into a serial killer, but often there was no physical cause for these behaviours. Wainewright seemed rather to be suffering from a lack of empathy, suggestive of a dissocial or antisocial personality, probably brought on by something that happened in his childhood.

As a psychiatrist, he would look in such a patient for anger brought on by a feeling of deprivation of love, or someone dying when he was young.

How closely Wainewright fits this diagnosis! His birth killed his mother, his father died while he was an infant leaving him to be brought up by a curmudgeonly grandfather in his seventies and his sharp-tongued grandmother, and provided for only grudgingly in the old man's will.

It was about this time in the early 19th century, said Dr Burns that attempts were made to separate out different mental disorders and consider treating them in different ways. In 1801 Phillipe Pinel published *Traité Médico-philosophique sur l'Aleniation Mentale; ou la Manie* in which he described "*manie sans delire*" - insanity without delusions.

This was defined in the 1830s as "moral insanity" by James Pritchard of Bristol Royal Infirmary in his *Treatise on Insanity and Other Disorders of the Mind*. The condition is neatly defined by *Duhaime's Law Dictionary* as a disease of the mind in which the individual is bereft of ethical judgment or feelings but still fully functioning intellectually. Later, it became relabelled as psychopathic personality. Here we have the template for a cold-blooded killer, possibly a poisoner, a crime regarded with particular horror because it is premeditated and usually achieved over a period by stealth, as the victim is gradually dosed to death. The *Times*, reflecting on the use of poisons for murder in 1865, wrote:

*The poisoner may be a smooth-faced plausible person, without any external symptoms of*

> *depravity, liable to no wild and furious outbursts of passion, imagining mischief secretly in the deep of his (sic) heart.*

Could this be Wainewright, never fully recovered from his great torments? He may well have stepped over that "brink of insanity" of which he wrote. Nevertheless, he went on to tell positively of his recovery from illness.

> *Two excellent secondary agents, a kind and skilful Physician and a most delicately-affectionate (though young and fragile) Nurse brought me at length out of those dead black waters, nearly exhausted with so sore a struggle.*

The nurse may have been his wife-to-be, Eliza, whose step-father, in one of the coincidences in the Wainewright story, was to die in the very barracks in Fermoy in which Wainewright had idled away his very brief military career.

He had not returned to Linden House after resigning his commission; perhaps the ignominy of doing so would have been too great and he would not have had so much of his highly-prized independence.

Instead he had taken lodgings in a boarding house run by a Mrs Frances Abercromby and her three young daughters at Mortlake, not far from Chiswick. It was a fateful day when Wainewright entered their lives. Two were to die suddenly and painfully.

Mrs Abercromby had married twice. Born Frances Weller, in Claygate, Surrey, she wedded in 1794 a widower named Cooper Ward. She was only 20, so had to have the consent of her father, a builder, which is noted in the Mortlake parish records. A son, John Cooper Ward, was born a year later, a daughter, Eliza Frances Ward, the future Mrs Wainewright, appeared in the summer of August 1796.

Cooper Ward was not long for this life, dying a few years later, leaving Frances in her twenties with two tiny children, but she soon married again, this time to an army officer, Lieut. John Bateman Abercromby. By him she had two further daughters, the first, Helen Frances Phoebe Abercromby, born in 1809, was to meet her untimely end in the Wainewright household under very strange circumstances. In 1810 she had a sister, burdened with the name Madalina Rosa Hibernia Burdett Abercromby, the Hibernia no doubt being imposed by her father who spent long periods in Ireland.

Lieut. Abercromby held his commission in the Royal Artillery Drivers, a small corps of the Royal Artillery which deployed gun carriages on the field of battle, for the army needed hundreds of horses to drag around the batteries of six-pound and three-pound guns.

It was not a sought-after section of the army in which to serve, for the Drivers had a dire reputation. Their antecedents were the scoundrel private contractors who had supplied horses to the artillery on the field of battle before the corps was founded in 1806, and who were known as being more likely to drive their charges away from the sound of gunfire as towards it.

Even after the Drivers became part of the army, military authorities of the time talked of them as being more interested in plunder than in their duty and of being the "scourge of the army". The officers, it was said, were seldom if ever with their men. Abercromby was commissioned as a second lieutenant in 1806 and bought his way to become a first lieutenant two years later, according to the *Army Lists* of the period.

Lieut. Abercromby served with a unit of the 6$^{th}$ Battalion Royal Artillery under the command of Captain Richard Dyas which had a strength of some 500 men - drivers, shoeing smiths, collar makers and veterinary surgeons. They had been for a number of years in Ireland, a fruitful source of supply for both men and horses, stationed mainly in Athlone, but on October 1st, 1811, they were re-deployed to Fermoy, where Wainewright was to serve.

Bateman Abercromby died suddenly that year, leaving Frances widowed a second time, with Bateman's two small daughters, their step-sister Eliza, now 15, and her brother John, who appears to drop out of the Abercromby story at this stage, possibly dying as a child. His mother was now even worse off than she was before. Her two daughters by Abercromby had been left by their father "not one shilling to save them from the workhouse" as a court was to hear many years later.

She had some income from a bequest of her father, freehold and leasehold property in Mortlake, which produced about £100 a year in rent, but it was not enough. She appealed to the Board of Ordnance for help in bringing up Bateman's two daughters and was granted an allowance of £10 a year for each until they were 21 years-old.

In the trials which were to follow, Lieut. Abercromby is several times described as a "meritorious officer" and there is one reference to his being killed in service, which he may have been, but not in the main British deployment of the time in the Peninsular Ward in Spain and Portugal as his name does not appear in the list of officers who served there.

Wainewright was not long in the boarding house at Mortlake, but long enough to decide to marry Eliza – an act he was later to describe as "injudicious". Six weeks or so after she became 21, and old enough to wed without consent, she and Wainewright, who was by now living in Craven Street, off the Strand, were married on November 13, 1817 by the curate at the nearby church of St Martin-in-the-Fields, overlooking what is now Trafalgar Square.

There was a marriage settlement dated the day before the wedding, altering the legacy from his grandfather. Wainewright would continue to draw the interest on the annuities, but after his death, his new wife and any children of the marriage would inherit.

One of the witnesses at the wedding was his cousin Edward Foss who he had recently painted in oils. A few years later he was to forge Foss's signature, defraud the Bank of England and set himself on the road to perdition.

## CHAPTER 4

## 'DIAMOND RINGS ON OUR FINGERS'

Wainewright recalled in one of his own essays for the *London Magazine* that his illness had prevented "steady pursuit", or work, as we know it, and "varied amusements" had been deemed essential to his cure, so it seems he spent some two years doing not very much other than painting and socialising.

There was never a better time in the 19th century to be a man-about-town than the age of the Regency dandy. According to Captain Gronow, that keen observer of the fashionable of the age, the dandy's dress in 1815 consisted of a blue coat with brass buttons, leather breeches and a huge white starched cravat, which forced the chin back at an almost impossible angle. Those with disappointing calves used padded inserts to enhance their showiness.

There is mention in one of Wainewright's essays of his wearing a blue coat and of wearing spurs on his heels during his society outings, a reference to his (failed) military career, of which he sometimes hinted of having been in a much more fashionable regiment than the infantry. Thomas Talfourd, Charles Lamb's biographer, who knew him and had dined at Linden House, described him as having a sort of "undress military air".

He was 5ft 6ins tall (1m 70cms), with a long nose and blue eyes, according to his application for a French passport in 1831. His hair was black, long, thick and curled and parted in the middle, according to his own description. He was said to stoop slightly and have a habit of lisping.

In the same description he talked of his "one large white hand decorated with regal rings". They are mentioned again in one of his essays:

*diamond rings on our fingers, the antique cameos in our breast-pins, our cambric pocket-handkerchief breathing forth attargul, our pale lemon-coloured kid gloves.*

John Clare, known as the Peasant Poet, whom Wainewright admired, was invited to dinner in February 1822 and wrote of him as "a very comical sort of chap. He is about 27 and wears a quizzing glass and makes an excuse for the ornament by complaining of bad eyes". Thomas Hood, another poet who was present, referred to Wainewright being "exquisitely scented and lisping". In the 1896 life of de Quincy by David Masson, Wainewright is referred to as "a shabby-genteel and bejewelled effeminate, whose department was the Fine Arts."

After his transportation to Van Diemen's Land, many of those who had enjoyed his hospitality were unsparing about his dandyism. He was, wrote the poet Barry Cornwall, "absolutely a fop, finikin in dress, with mincing steps and tremulous words, with his hair curled and full of unguents and his cheeks painted like those of a frivolous demi-rep", defined at that time as 'a woman of uncertain virtue'. Talfourd said his conversation was that of "smart, lively, clever, heartless, voluptuous coxcomb".

"He is ubiquitous" wrote Walter Thornbury. "Go to the Park and you observe him in his phaeton, leaning forward with his cream-coloured gloves and his large turned-down wristbands conspicuous over the splashboard. Go to old Lady Fitzrattle's ball the same evening and you will see the fascinating creature with the belle of the evening, gracefully revolving in the waltz". Hardly a contemporary description, it was written more than 20 years after his death.

Wainewright was a dandy, but not like the rather dim Regency buffs whose horizons were bounded by Grosvenor Square and St James' and who spent vast amounts on gambling and on amusing themselves at Almanack's Assembly Rooms, a marriage mart for the aristocracy.

His was an artistic dandyism, a posturing to draw attention to himself and his talents rather than to impress other followers of fashion. As Baudelaire, himself a dandy, wrote: "Dandyism is not an excessive delight in clothes and material elegance. For the perfect dandy, these are no more than a symbol of the aristocratic superiority of the mind."

Wainewright had no doubt about the latter as far as he was concerned. He knew Latin and Greek, French and German, had an encyclopaedic knowledge of art and a keen eye as an artistic and literary critic.

It was the height of Romanticism in art and literature, the era of Turner, Constable and Fuseli, of Wordsworth, Blake, Coleridge, Shelley, Keats and others. Their emphasis on the beauties of nature and the importance of emotion and the self, rather than dictates of reason and order promoted by the 18th century Enlightenment, was a cause that Wainewright enthusiastically embraced, as

Many Regency artists, including Turner and Fuseli produced, for private viewing, portfolios of erotic drawings. Wainewright did the same. One of his that still exists is this sepia line and wash version of Lady passing two lovers on a bank embracing.

*British Museum*

he did their espousal of the irrational, mystical and supernatural.

As well as some minor writings, he seems to have become involved in producing the catalogue for the Royal Academy exhibitions, which would have brought him into contact with the London artists of the day. One of their social gatherings which he attended was at the premises of Paul Colnaghi, print-seller to the Prince Regent, who was in business with his sons Dominic and Martin. They held court monthly in their large room at Cockspur Street. Artists and politicians attended too, and the atmosphere was said to like that of a gentleman's club.

There was an unsubstantiated tale, put forward by Barry Cornwall, that Wainewright had acquired expensive prints which contained Colnaghi's pricing on their cardboard mounts, then substituted much cheaper prints and sold them on for great profit. The Colnaghi archive, which is held at Waddesdon Manor, the home of the Rothschilds, is, alas, incomplete, and contains no record of Wainewright's dealings.

John Scott, the writer and critic who had revived the London Magazine in 1820, had married Colnaghi's daughter Caroline in 1807. The *London* rapidly gained ascendancy in the literary world by publishing the works of Wordsworth, Charles Lamb, Carlyle and John Clare among others. Notable contributions were Thomas de Quincey's *Confessions of an English Opium Eater* and William Hazlitt's essay in 1822 on the Elgin Marbles.

It is probably through the Colnaghi connection that Wainewright was commissioned to write for the *London,* as Scott had noted his artistic enthusiasm. He recalled in one of the essays:

> *It struck me as something ridiculous that I, who had never authorized a line, save in Orderly and Guard reports (and letters for money of course) should be considered competent to appear in a new double-good Magazine!*
>
> *I actually laughed outright to the consternation of my cat and dog, who wondered, I believe, what a plague ailed me.*

Contributors to magazines in the 19th century usually adopted *noms-de-plume*. Wainewright used a telling one, Janus Weathercock, the two-faced

Roman god, and one who could be blown in any direction. The other name he used, purporting to be a Dutchman, was Cornelius Van Vinkbooms, a surname probably appropriated from David Vinckbooms (sic), one of the painters of the Dutch Golden Age, who was greatly influenced by Breughel the Elder.

In the three years from February 1820 Wainewright contributed some 15 attributable essays to the *London*.[1] Several of them are devoted to his expensive possessions and extravagant lifestyle; de Quincey, his fellow contributor, was not convinced by this showiness:

> *(He) could not conceal the ostentatious pleasure which he took in the luxurious fittings-up of his rooms, in the fancied splendour of his bijouterie, &c. Yet it was easy for a man of any experience to read two facts in all this idle etalage (display); one being, that his finery was but of a second-rate order; the other, that he was a parvenu, not at home even amongst his second-rate splendour.*

Wainwright's striving for effect in his essays makes some of them quite difficult to read today, though his

---

[1.] Carew Hazlitt also attributes to Wainewright two articles in the *London* signed "Egomet Bonmot Esq." which Hazlitt added to the known works as he detected a similarity of style. This attribution has recently been disputed by Marc Vaulbert de Chantilly, who says they are probably the work of another contributor, Edward Gandy. *"Some passages" in the Life &c of Egonmet Bonmot, Esq.* The Vanity Press of Bethnal Green. 2000.

criticisms of artistic exhibitions are easier. Turner, for instance, "has great dashing faults which would sink an ordinary artist"; He was almost reverential about his friend Sir Thomas Lawrence, the leading portraitist of his day and president of the Royal Academy, whose "breadth, richness and depth" he praised. The poet Swinburne called Wainewright the finest English art critic before John Ruskin, whose monumental five-volume *Modern Painters* defined the way Victorians thought of art.

But the other essays are mainly self-referential whimsy, showing off his knowledge and with more than a dash of parody, and it is likely that Scott recruited him to the *London* to leaven the otherwise serious content of the magazine. "Clever, but very fantastical essays as a relief from the more serious papers of his other friends", said Cornwall.

As Wainewright said in his first essay, he had agreed with Scott that he should be allowed to be as profound or as flighty, as serious or as comical, as he pleased. Friends like Clare thought his contributions "very entertaining" and Lamb referred to him as "Kind light-hearted Wainwright (sic)...a genius of the Lond. Mag."

By the time his last essay, *The Weathercock Steadfast for Lack of Oil* appeared in January 1823, the magazine was on the downward slope. Poor Scott had not lived to see much of its short-lived success. A bitter literary feud with a contributor to another magazine led to a duel by moonlight at 9pm on February 27, 1821. A bullet went through his intestines and he died nine days later at his lodgings in Covent Garden. Wainewright was to write melodramatically that he was with

The Royal Academy summer exhibitions at Somerset House were one of the social highlights of Georgian and Regency London. This Cruickshank caricature is of the 1821 exhibition in which Wainewright's work was first shown.

*British Museum*

him towards the end. "I feel...round my neck the heart-breaking, feeble, kindly clasp of his fever-wasted arm - his faint whisper of entire trust in my friendship (though short)".

As his literary efforts petered out, he turned much more to his painting, which flowered between 1821 and 1825, when he exhibited six paintings at the Royal Academy, then based in Somerset House in the Strand, where the summer exhibition was one of the highlights of the London social season.

In 1821 he showed the *Romance from Undine*, one of his favourite subjects. That year's show was caricatured by Isaac and George Cruickshank in their etching "*A shilling well laid out*" which shows the fashionable crowds thronging the Great Room looking at the pictures; Wainewright's effort is not among those displayed.

He then showed in the following year *Paris in the Chamber of Helen*, then *The Milkmaid's Song* (1824), and two in 1825, *Sketch from La Gerusalemme Liberata* and *Scene from Der Freischütz*. Two of them were indebted to the German Romantic movement that he admired so much.

*The Milkmaid's Song*, was praised at the 1824 exhibition by William Blake who declared it "very fine". All were hung where lesser artists were displayed, well "above the line". This was a wooden moulding running around the Great Room at Somerset House at a height of about eight feet. Large works and those of celebrated artists' works sat on the line.

None of Wainewright's exhibits is known to survive. Despite having exhibited six pictures and applied for one of the three vacancies to become an Associate Member of the Academy, he failed to receive a single vote. This is surprising, given his closeness to Sir Thomas Lawrence and the Academy's Professor of Painting and Keeper, the Swiss-German artist John Henry Fuseli. Indeed, he was in a special carriage with Lawrence in the funeral procession as they followed Fuseli's lead-lined coffin to St Paul's Cathedral.

Wainewright was a passionate admirer of Fuseli, whose 1782 painting of Gothic horror *The Nightmare* - a study of a supine woman upon whom is seated a malevolent imp - created a sensation, as did many of his later supernatural works. Wainewright was so close to Fuseli that one of the

Abercromby sisters - it is not known which - sat in his studio in the cellars of Somerset House for his 1821 painting *Undine Comes into the House of the Fishermen,* a less-than flattering depiction of a rather gawky-looking young girl in white entering a dark, threatening room.

The event was recorded by an American artist, Mary Balmanno, in her reminiscences, *Pen and Pencil.* As Mrs Fuseli moved forward to talk to her husband "two very pretty girls sprang forward and saluted her; they were the sisters Helen and Madeleine (sic), one of whom had been sitting for the portrait of Undine." Helen would have been 11 at the time, Madalina a year younger.

The picture, which has Fuseli's dark notes of the supernatural, is based on a German fairy tale in which Undine, a water spirit, meets the knight, Huldebrand in the fisherman's house and marries him so that she can gain a soul. The tale also fascinated Wainewright, two of the pictures he exhibited at the Academy - in 1821 and 1823 - were based upon the story.

Fuseli also produced highly-erotic drawings, as did other Regency artists, including J M W Turner.[2] Wainewright's own sepia line and wash *Lady passing two lovers on a bank embracing* is

---

[2.] The prissy art critic John Ruskin, Turner's executor, going through the artist's effects in 1858, was horrified to discover a large number of highly erotic paintings and drawings. He maintained that he had made a bonfire of them as Turner was obviously insane when he did them. However in 2005 large numbers of them were identified in the Tate Britain archive.

in the Print Room of the British Museum.[3] The *Dictionary of National Biography* refers to it sniffily as "coarse and indelicate, but by no means lacking in technical skill".

It probably formed part of a portfolio he had of such drawings, done for the benefit of his friends. Lamb's biographer Talfourd reported that these sketches "trembled on the borders of indelicate". Carew Hazlitt called them exquisite delineations of the female form, which, regarded from an unprofessional point of view, might have been characterised as decidedly erotic and reminded him of the "famous leg-comparing episode" in the memoirs of the Duc de Grammont.[4]

Wainewright was a passionate collector of rare books, prints and *objets d'art,* which he itemised at length in one of his essays as "Janus's Jumble". "My tables groan with the weight of volumes of Raffaëlle, Michel Angelo, Rubens, Poussin, Parmegiano, Giulio &c. &c. and the massive portfolio cases open wide their doors, disclosing yet fresh treasures within". The binding of one of the books alone cost him 12 guineas (nearly £1.500). There was a small Book of Hours, a Christian devotional book said to have belonged to Anne Boleyn, studded with brilliants

---

[3.] Period VI, vol 79

[4.] The French King Charles II and his court, having little else to do, were discussing the short and thick legs of Lady Chesterfield, when the King persuaded a Miss Stuart to raise her skirt above the knee for comparison purposes, "which she did with the greatest imaginable ease ". Most were ready to prostrate themselves to adore their beauty, Grammont reported. Hamilton, A. *Memoirs of the Court of Charles the Second.* Bohn, London, 1846.

and rubies. There are lists of other precious objects, bronzes, prints and fine furniture.

But where had all the money come from for this treasure trove?

## CHAPTER 5

## THE BANK OF ENGLAND SWINDLED!

An income of £250 a year from the trust fund allowed for a fairly expansive lifestyle, compared with the wages of less than a fifth of that on which artisans and manual workers were bringing up families. But for Wainewright and Eliza, grandfather Ralph's grudging benison was never going to be enough. Money was to be begged, borrowed and stolen to fund their huge expenses.

In 1821, they had moved to one of central London's most fashionable addresses, Great Marlborough Street, laid out in the early 18th Century, "inhabited all by fine Quality" and "one of the finest streets in Europe"[1]. At No.49, where they took an apartment, had lived the both the Earls of Sutherland and of Bute, and the actress Sarah Siddons.

It was a large four-storey building divided into apartments around a square central well around which rose an elegant staircase. The Wainewrights appear to have rented the apartment on the top floor, for he talks in one of his essays of "Janus's

---

[1] Survey of London. London County Council, 1963. Vol xxxxi, p.24. The area became known for its artists. At No. 49 In 1834, was another painter and exhibitor at the Academy, one A. Morton, followed by Charles Hullmandel, artist and print-maker. Later it became the Fine Arts Institute Nos. 49 and 50 were demolished in 1884 to make way for the church of St John the Baptist which itself was demolished in 1937. There is now an office block on the site.

boudoir", an octagon of 13 feet in diameter into which the light streams though rosy panes in the dome above, there being no other windows. Not a sound from the street reaches it. The walls are covered with very rich crimson French paper, formed into panels with gold mouldings and the oak floor is spread with a glowing Persian carpet on which rests a pomona-green Morocco *chaise-longue*. In this room are all his treasures.

Was Wainewright in these descriptions exaggerating his sybaritic lifestyle and striving for effect? Possibly, but there was no doubt about his extravagance. "Far from being prudent and thrifty, he loved carriages, majolica, rare prints, wines of unusual vintages, servants in livery and other sweet impoverishments", wrote Carew Hazlitt disapprovingly.

It was at Great Marlborough Street that he entertained lavishly his literary and artistic friends and lived the life of a London dilettante which he related in one of his essays:

> *I enter with great gusto into the amusements of town. I see all new exhibitions; hear all new singers; frequent the sacred Argyll, the Cyder Cellar, the Opera, Long's, Colnaghi's and the Coal Hole. I rummage carefully the catalogue... for old bokes (sic), write articles and inspect one magazine (the London).*

But the cost of high living in a lavish apartment in the heart of London's West End and his magpie acquisition of expensive *objets d'art* was leading to crushing debts. Wainewright's only income other than the interest from his grandfather's will was and whatever pittance he got for his occasional writings and articles in the *London Magazine*. His last article had appeared in January 1823.

To pay off his debts and to continue funding his extraordinary lifestyle he took the first step in an audacious fraud that was to lead to his banishment to the other end of the world.

On May 12, 1823, he went into the Bank of England with a power of attorney that entitled him to withdraw a lump sum of £2,250 in New 4% annuities from the trust fund left by his grandfather. The annuities had been converted only ten days previously from the original Navy 5% of £5,000 and were now worth £5,250.

But the power of attorney was completely bogus and the signatures of the three trustees - all his relations - were forged by Wainewright, as were the made-up names and signatures of the witnesses to the signing of the power of attorney.

The document[2] said that Robert Wainewright of Grays Inn, Edward Smith Foss of Essex Street, Strand and Edward Foss of Russell Square "all in Middlesex, Esquires" had appointed Thomas Griffiths Wainewright of Great Marlborough Street, Artist, as their attorney to sell, assign and transfer all or any part of the £2,250. One of the Bank's clerks, a Mr Catteron, witnessed the transfer and half of his grandfather's bequest was handed over.

Wainewright was to argue later, quite speciously, that it was his money after all and he was entitled

---
[2] National Archives. Crim4/64

The forged signatures of the trustees and the fictional witnesses on the power of attorney that enabled the heavily-indebted Wainewright to defraud the Bank of England and drain the last of his grandfather's bequest before fleeing to France.

*National Archives*

to it, but this was a blatant fraud against the Bank, for as long as the Bank held the trust fund it was accountable for it.

The Bank's own inflation calculator puts the value of this in 2017 as an astonishing £245,000, but reckless expense and debt soon dissipated this enormous sum.

But then he must have thought that having got away with swindling the Bank of England once, he could do successfully do it again.

A year later, almost to the day, on May 17, 1824, Wainewright was back at the Bank with another power of attorney. Again the signatures of the trustees were forged and again the witnesses were bogus.

The Bank made no checks and paid out £3,000 (£302.000), which enabled him to drain entirely his grandfather's trust fund. There was now nothing left for Eliza after his death or for any child of their marriage. But then he and Eliza had been married for several years, and there was no sign of any offspring.

He was, however, taking a terrible risk, the penalty for such forgery was death by public execution, and a few months after his last visit to the Bank came a *cause célèbre* which must have caused him considerable disquiet - the case of the city banker Henry Fauntleroy, who had also forged powers of attorney and defrauded the Bank of England, just as Wainewright had done.

Newspaper stories reported Fauntleroy's dissolute life with vast sums spent on women and gambling. But a confession found in a tin box at the bank in which he was a partner, said he had done it to keep his own bank going and blamed the Bank of England for rejecting his payments and refusing him credit. "They shall smart for it", he wrote. The confession was found by Freshfields the Bank of England solicitors, who were to pursue Wainewright many years later.

On November 2, 1824, at the Old Bailey, Fauntleroy was convicted of forging powers of attorney to secure £170,000, though the real figure was said to be £400,000. The case attracted enormous public attention and sympathy for Fauntleroy, but despite 16 character witnesses, he was sentenced to death and on November 30 he was hanged in front of the debtor's door at Newgate Prison.

There had been a series of petitions and appeals to no avail; an Italian was said to have offered to take his place on the scaffold; another tale said he had inserted a silver tube in his throat and escaped death - hardly likely as it was an execution before a crowd estimated at 100,000 people; public executions were common in England until 1866.

Charles Lamb, writing after the execution, and quoted by Carew Hazlitt, said pointedly that it had made him cast reflecting eyes on such of his friends in a parity of situation, all exposed to a similarity of temptation. As a friend and admirer of Wainewright, perhaps he had his own suspicions.

For prodigious spending soon exhausted the illicit sums from the Bank and by 1826, Wainewright was borrowing heavily from a solicitor friend, John Atkinson, who was exacting unusual terms. To guarantee an existing loan of £3,000 and to secure a further £1,500, Wainewright agreed to pay Atkinson and several of his relatives £150 a year for their lives, and to the end of the life of the last survivor. He had to give as security books, engravings and pictures which were kept in boxes by another solicitor, Robert Shank Acheson. This was to be followed by a series of other loans, warrants of attorney and stratagems to keep the Wainewrights afloat.

There was no hope now of an artistic career; the slender talent of the precious young man who had delighted literary London ten years before had burned itself out; and in painting there was no prospect that he would have a fashionable studio in the West End to which society would flock.

It was obvious that the seven years of high living at Great Marlborough Street had to come to an end. In the autumn of 1827, the Wainewrights forsook the expensive West End to move to the rustic grandeur of Linden House in Chiswick to live with uncle George. Whether he invited them or whether they foisted themselves upon him is not known. But once they were ensconced there, uncle George's days were numbered.

# CHAPTER 6

# SUDDEN DEATHS AT LINDEN HOUSE

Uncle George had sold the *Monthly Review* in 1825 and retired to potter in the grounds of Linden House and tend his beloved gardens, but his retirement was short-lived once the Wainewrights had arrived. He died in convulsive agony in January 1828 and was buried on the 24th at Turnham Green. He was only 56. His death had been witnessed by the doctor's old servant, and Wainewright's nurse, Sarah Handcocks, who was to tell of it later as coincidences began to mount.

Some sources put the date of George's death as January 16th; if so it was an extraordinary day at Linden House. For Eliza, after nearly 10 years of marriage, had given birth to a boy on the same day. He was called Griffiths - named after his mother, grandfather and great-uncle.

The birth date appears in the records of St Nicholas Church, Chiswick, but young Griffiths was a long time being christened. It was nearly six months later, on June 4, that the ceremony took place. The delay was unusual and so possibly was the parentage itself.

Wainewright was to write in one of his several petitions for clemency that in 1823, when the first forgeries took place, after six years of marriage, he... "neither had or (sic) was likely to have Children".

Suddenly he had a son. Many years later there was gossip, mainly fomented by his erstwhile friend Barry Cornwall, that the real father was a "dissipated and impoverished peer", though this has never been substantiated, and Wainewright would hardly have named the child after himself if he suspected he had been cuckolded, though Eliza herself was to prove less than trustworthy, and indeed deadly, in other matters.

However, the birth records show that Eliza and Wainewright - who is described in the column for Quality, Trade or Profession as "Esquire" - were the parents of the hapless Griffiths, whose childhood was to be ruined by Wainewright's actions.

He was now the owner of the magnificent Linden House and another £5,000, for bachelor Uncle George had died without bothering to make a will and Wainewright was the only living relative. Dr Griffiths had not wanted to leave a penny more to his grandson than he had settled on his daughter, but now the dissipated dandy had inherited the lot – the huge house, its contents, horses and carriages - and cash.

Wainewright might have expected even more, but the *Monthly Review* had been loss-making and the costs of running a large country house were huge. He was now living in his usual high style, this time as a country gentleman, but he had inherited a white elephant which would make his problems much worse.

In April, he began selling off the library at Linden House, including around a thousand volumes of the newspapers and magazines that George Griffiths and his father had used in editing the *Monthly Review*. Rare books, pictures, music and casts were to follow. Notable among them were 200 volumes of the *Monthly Review*, the editors' set; Sir Thomas Lawrence's portrait of Dr Ralph Griffiths, pictures by Fuseli and Richard Westall and Wainewright's *Scene from Walton's Angler*. A huge amount was sold over the course of the next year or so, but Wainewright was not to benefit. Whatever was raised was already spoken for in paying off his debts.

The auctioneer was Benjamin Wheatley, who had substantial premises in Piccadilly. He was a widower with children, who was to become Wainewright's brother-in-law, for while cataloguing the contents of Linden House before the auctions, he had met Madalina Abercromby, then 19 years old, and in May 1832 he was to marry her.

Madalina, her sister Helen and their mother had moved to Linden House to be with Wainewright and Eliza from Sheen, where they had been teetering on edge of genteel poverty. Eliza's mother, Frances, despite her small property holdings in Mortlake, where they had recently lived, was so short of money that she had borrowed £200 from John Stuart, the auctioneer who collected her rents. When her properties finally had to be sold in 1829, she still owed him £40, which he was never to receive.

But she must have been delighted to move to such a fashionable address, to which the cream of artistic London, such as Charles Lamb and the famous actor-manager Charles Macready still came to dine; Wainewright's artistic talents might have forsaken him through idleness, but he was a witty host who entertained lavishly and kept at his dinner table a vicarious hold of his former life.

Now even this was threatened. The local tradesmen were owed hundreds of pounds - credit on a scale almost unthinkable today - and the supplies of even the staples of life could not be guaranteed for very much longer.

The only person in the household who had any was Mrs Abercromby. She had been left a small sum and some rental income by her late husband, but this was pitifully little. However, poor as she was, she made a will on August 13th 1829, leaving everything she had to her eldest daughter Eliza, wife, as the document says, of Thomas Griffiths Wainewright - he who would have persuaded her not only to make the will but to make him the sole executor. It was witnessed by Sarah Handcocks, who was to see her die within the week.

She, Helen and Madalina watched the course of the sudden illness that killed Mrs Abercromby in her mid-fifties. Sarah was to claim much later that if followed a path of vomiting, violent convulsions, then death, much like Uncle George's the previous year.

In the 1894 edition of the *Dictionary of National Biography*, where Wainewright's life is chronicled - to some extent inaccurately - by Thomas Seccombe, there is a suggestion that Mrs Abercromby had objected to Wainewright's plans to insure Helen's life for suspicious purposes and that this had dramatically shortened her own. To die within seven days of making a will, where none had existed before, should have raised the alarm, but her death went unremarked. As to her relatively young age, the average life expectancy at the time was in the mid-thirties, but this figure is heavily skewed due to the huge incidence of infant mortality in the 19th century.

The course of Mrs Abercromby's illness, its swiftness and fatality, was to be duplicated a few months later, and in that case there is now little doubt that poison was responsible. Whatever her motives for making a will, her death was doubly fortunate for Wainewright. It enabled Eliza to receive a small bequest of £100 to ease the family's financial burdens and, without benefit of mother-in-law, allowed a bold scheme for alleviating Wainewright's chronic shortage of money to be put into place.

In the meantime, any little sum helped. Helen, who had come of age on March 12 1830 wrote from Linden House in August to the Board of Ordnance asking for the pension of £10 a year which she had had since the death of her father in 1811 to be continued, as it had expired when she reached 21. The letter is written from beginning to end without a full stop as if it had been dashed off without thought – or perhaps had been taken down verbatim while it was being dictated by her relatives:

> ...(I) have attained the age of 21 years, am totally unprovided for, being also deprived of the support of my mother who died August last, and require the continuance of the assistance of the Honourable Board whom I trust will take my case into consideration and direct that the allowance may be continued to me for which I shall be ever grateful.
>
> I have the Honor (sic) to be Sir, Your very humble servant
> Helen Abercromby

The Board agreed that the Bounty, as they called it, should continue, but first they needed an affidavit from Helen as to her circumstances. She swore it at the Hatton Garden police office on October 20,

The Bounty would never be paid – she had only two months to live.

## CHAPTER 7

## THE INSURANCE FRAUDS

It must have been at this point that the Wainewrights realized that there would have to be another fraud; it was the only way in which large sums of money could be obtained quickly enough to pay off the most pressing debtors and ensure the continuity of life at Linden House.

The Bank of England forgeries had now remained undetected for six and more years. If an august and secure body like the Bank could be duped, it would be relatively easy to deceive other institutions with large amounts of capital - insurance companies for instance and although such a plan would involve more risks, the rewards would be so much greater.

The details fell neatly into place. The life of Eliza's sister, Helen Abercromby, could be insured for a short period, then perhaps she could leave the country and the insurance companies could be persuaded that she was dead - and forced to disgorge. Alternatively, she could be done away with...

Helen became 21, old enough to sign papers on her own behalf, on March 12, 1830. She was a bright, energetic girl and handsome, one witness was to say, though Wainwright's crayon drawing of her as a young girl a few years earlier fails to do justice to the description. For insurance purposes she was ideal - young and healthy.

Laying the groundwork carefully, note had to be made of her good constitution. Wainewright's surgeon friend in Turnham Green, Dr. Thomas Graham, examined her and declared her "an excellent life" for insuring.

The records of Helen's insurances are well-documented. The original company policy papers have long since disappeared though some scanty board minutes survive. The evidence itself comes from two trials in the Court of the Exchequer which took place in 1835, which show clearly the extent of the desperate fraud - and how unlikely it was to succeed.

The cases were brought to try to force the insurance companies to pay up and were reported extensively in the *Times, Morning Post, Morning Chronicle*[1] and other newspapers, from which these accounts are drawn.

The audacious scheme, which was to involve eight different insurance companies, began within days of Helen's 21st birthday. She was taken on a bewildering round of London life assurance offices by Wainewright and Eliza. In all, Helen made 15 visits to insurance offices between March and October 1830. In almost all of them it was Eliza who accompanied her and did a lot of the talking.

In the 18th century there had been very few life assurance companies in London, but by the 1830s the number had grown substantially and there was stiff competition for premiums. The Alliance, for instance, one of the offices on the grand tour, had been founded only six years previously.

The first call was at the Palladium on March 23rd 1830; it had also been founded for only six years,

---

[1] Issues of June 30, 1835 and December 4, 1835.

and there an application was made for a policy on Helen's life for £3,000

Two days later Wainewright took her to the Pelican Office in Spring Gardens. This time the sum insured was £5,000. Next on March 26, it was the Eagle's turn. By tradition the chief executive of a life insurance company was called the actuary and the Eagle's actuary, Henry P Smith was to become Wainewright's nemesis.

The proposal was made for an insurance on her life for £3,000, acceptance subject to a medical report, which of course had already been procured. Dr Graham was able to certify that not only was she healthy when she was examined, he had never known her to have a day's illness in her life.

At life offices in several parts of London, clerks and officials were to deal with Miss Helen Frances Phoebe Abercromby's applications for policies. There was one common factor, apart from the unusual number of them, they were all very short term, for only two years or, as in the case of the Palladium, three. An ideal prospect for the insurance companies - for why should a healthy young woman die within two or three years?

On April 20th, Eliza took Helen to the Palladium office again. The actuary, Nicholas Grute, showed understandable curiosity. Why was the insurance for so short a period? Eliza had a ready answer. It was to raise money to enable the family to get possession of property which would fall in within three years. In other words the policy could be used as security to raise money; if Helen died in the meantime, the loan would be paid off with the insurance.

Helen, who had declared herself to be a year older than she really was, had the same question asked. She could not give any reason - apparently the business of property settlement was a bit over her head. The only answer she gave was that she had been told "it was proper" for her to do it.

This procedure of insuring for a short term to raise money against a policy was not uncommon. In September 1834, for instance, the Eagle accepted a proposal for a loan of £12,000 to be raised against the life of John Cochrane - again just 21 - who was to become entitled to a large sum of money on attaining the age of 25; if he died before then the money would go to someone else. Several other life offices accepted the proposal. Alas, very shortly afterwards, as the Eagle minutes report, poor Cochrane took an open carriage from Boulogne to Calais in the teeth of a cold north-easterly wind and died in no time at all of inflammation of various organs.

Nevertheless Grute of the Palladium was a trusting man for an insurance official. There seems to have been no attempt at this stage by him, or any of the other insurers who were to be gulled, to make any attempt to verify the truth of the property bequest; perhaps the pressure to bring in the premiums led to carelessness. So despite evasive and inconclusive explanations Grute accepted the risk. Helen signed the policy and paid the premium of £39 plus £4 stamp duty - money which had come from the slim pocket of her brother-in-law.

Her life - or rather her death - had suddenly become worth a great deal of money. Ten days later it was worth double; she signed policy number 80230 at the Eagle and again paid the hefty premium and stamp duty on the spot.

Her death within three years would now bring in vast sums, considerably more than Wainewright had swindled from the Bank, and enough to pay off all the debts and live in the lavish style he craved. But it was still not enough - not for the risks that had to be taken.

If two companies had issued the policies, how many more would do so if he could keep on putting up £40 a time? This was the only difficulty - he hadn't the resources to do so. There came a lull in the insurance business, and a death in a distant part of the family.

Edward Smith Foss, the eldest of the trustees died in May. Wainewright attended the funeral of the man whose signature he had twice forged, and wrote a letter of condolence to his son, also named Edward, who was again an unconscious victim of his penmanship:

> *Dear Cousin*
> *I was not surprised yet much shocked by your news. A truly kind and good friend has been taken; one of those old hearts (English to the core) that yet remained in a generation of frost and pretence. You will, I know, bear yourself a rational man though the blank will press heavily at your house of solitary business. 'I will go and ask my father!' - but his desk is empty. There is no man I esteemed like your father and I cherished a hope to show myself to him in a new light; my disappointment is more than you can perhaps give credit for.*

> *Your mournful compliment in allowing my attendance at the last parting of his earthly remains was duly felt - Good God! It seems only a month since I stood with him the in pit to hear Kean in Hamlet. But we get older ourselves; and every season will steal away some of the old familiar faces, till comes our own wintry night. My poor cousins are good and pious and doubtless look for another meeting in eternity. How must such hope lighten the heavy grief. I have no such hope!*
>
> *Yet just God has given me in its stead full reliance on his now inscrutable dispensation. Do we really individually exist? Are we? or is matter nothing but an idea? This life a swoon of the spirit and the grave a wakening? But the Lord of the Sun and Stars is good! May he comfort you all.*
>
> *T.G.W.*[2]

An uncharacteristic note of sincerity has stolen in, another side of personality revealed. A troubled man pondering on the ultimate; reliant on "inscrutable dispensation" - this for the wrong he had done, or was about to do?

Despite the companionable trips to the theatre, the old man must have noted Wainewright closely. There is the give-away phrase: "I had hoped to show myself to him in a new light."

But the mood of sobriety did not last. Wainewright's debtors were becoming tired of waiting for their money. The most persistent of his creditors was,

---
[2.] Quoted by Curling. p.229

Murdered to pay off enormous debts. The unfortunate Helen Abercromby as a child, drawn in crayon by Wainewright.

of course, a moneylender, the curiously-named Sharpus of Cockspur Street, who was owed more than £600 under a warrant of attorney.

On July 8th, Sharpus claimed his due and a bill of sale was made out on all the furnishing and fittings of Linden House against which Wainewright had borrowed money. The money would have fallen due on Midsummer Day, one of the four Quarter Days in the year when significant debts were settled.

The following month the £610 was due; Wainewright could not pay and applied for more time, Sharpus agreed and the day of reckoning was postponed until December 21. This date was to be crucial. To secure the extension Wainewright swore an affidavit that he had pledged his securities to no-one else, which was untrue. Money without security he owed to the friends he had left - to one of them, Madalina's future husband, he owed £200.

On September 25 1830, almost four months since the last policy had been effected, the visits to the insurance companies began again. Wainewright visited the Pelican, where enquiries had been made in March, to ask further about a policy worth £5,000 on Helen's life, this time for only two years. It was accepted on October 8.

He was followed to the office by Eliza and Helen, who completed the policy; Helen paid over the premium one £50 and a £10 note. These notes were to become important later, as they could be traced directly to Wainewright. Helen was now worth £11,000 - dead.

Then there came two setbacks within a week of each other. Actuaries in two different companies were rather more cautious about the explanations put forward by Eliza and Helen. There was more than a suspicion that they were not acting with what insurance companies call *uberrima fides* - the best of faith.

On October 1, 1830 Helen visited the Globe Insurance company and proposed that they should insure her for £5,000 for two years. She visited the office a second time accompanied by Eliza.

Why, she was asked by the company secretary, John Charles Denham, did she wish to insure her life? She showed the same reluctance to answer as she had at the Palladium. "I don't know, I am desired to do it". She was asked again, but could say no more. Perhaps her step-sister could explain?

Eliza dismissed the matter airily: "It is so. There are some money matters to be arranged. Ladies do not know much about those things".

Denham persisted and put a direct question to Helen - one to which he already knew the answer: Was she arranging policies with any other insurance companies? Her answer was equally direct: "No".

This was a mistake, for by now the insurance companies were talking to each other; Denham had already contacted some of the other companies and knew there were policies in place. He knew Helen was lying and was readily able to turn down the premium of £60, with the prospect of losing £5,000.

The half-sisters were not daunted; four days later they were at the Alliance in Bartholomew Lane. Helen was now primed with more details of the plausible tale, almost certainly concocted by Wainewright and Eliza, who would not have known that it was the lie that caught out Helen at the Globe, rather than a lack of explanation for her actions.

She told the secretary, Andrew Hamilton, that a suit was pending in Chancery which would probably end soon in her favour. But there was a snag: if she were to die in the meantime the property would go to another family. Would the Alliance cover her for £5,000 for two years to cover this unlikely contingency, so that her family would not lose?

Hamilton was even more wary than Denham, for the Globe had not been the only company to contact other insurers. He questioned Helen closely until she burst out: "I thought your enquiries would be about my health and not about the object that I have in insuring".

Hamilton had a cautionary tale to tell: a young lady had come to the office about two years before to insure her life for a short period. She had died - the company believed by unfair means - and there was now more caution about such short-term insurances. In a phrase of dreadful irony Helen replied: "I am sure that no person about me could have such an object." Hamilton agreed, but the Alliance would not accept the risk.

On then to the Imperial on October 14, the sum scaled down to £3,000, possibly in the hope that the lower the sum assured, the fewer the questions. There was another questioning of intent, by the company's actuary, Samuel Ingall. Did she want the insurance to secure property which would come to her at the end of two years?

Eliza replied that Helen wanted to provide for her sister Madalina and would be able to do so from other sources after two years. She had not insured with any other office and they would return to sign the papers. However, they really needed to insure her for £5,000, so they were going to find the additional £2,000 in cover elsewhere.

Part of this was true, for the following day the two were back at the Eagle offices, asking for the existing policy of £3,000 to be increased by another £2,000. The Eagle declined. The same day, they went on to the Hope, who did accept, after a medical examination, a proposal for £2,000.

Back then to Imperial on October 20 and some disquieting news; Ingall had discovered that there was already a policy for £5,000 in operation with another company and she had been rejected by a further life office. He was to testify five years later that he said to her: "I am instructed by the directors to say they are very much displeased".

What other policies had been taken out was relevant to whether the directors would accept the risk on her life. "She appeared very much agitated", said Ingall. Helen was all innocence; she said she understood very little of the matter. "I do as my friends direct me".

Ingall must have been convinced; despite the evidence of mendacity he relented and issued Imperial policy number 1119. Three thousand pounds would be paid if death occurred within two years. Eliza paid the premium of £44. (Short-term insurance was expensive; the Imperial would have charged only £66 to insure her for life.)

There was a final one more speculation on October 19, 1830; the Provident was prepared to issue a policy for £2,000 and the company's director Barber Beaumont declared Helen to be "a remarkably healthy, cheerful and handsome-looking woman." But the premium was never paid - the money had run out.

Helen Abercromby worth £10 a year alive was now worth £16,000 dead. This was a colossal sum in 1830. There are various online calculators which can translate this into 2017 values, but they vary widely, the Bank of England's own inflation calculator, for instance, puts the sum at more than £3million, another suggests £1,300,000.

How had Helen been persuaded to connive in such a scheme? Did she not realise that her life was in the balance? What had Wainewright and Eliza told her about the possible outcome of the escapade? She must have known that the story of great expectations from a suit in Chancery was a lie, but may she have been convinced that a disappearance abroad was a possibility.

At the last insurance office she had been agitated, because she had been caught out in a lie; she must surely have realised that she whatever the possible outcome, she was involved in a large-scale deception.

But it is not unknown for a woman to be deluded into co-operating in her own murder. The curious case in the 19th century of the Parisian homeopathic doctor Couty de la Pommerais bears some similarity to Wainewright's exploits. He, too, killed for gain, attempted to defraud insurance companies and disposed of his mother-in-law.

The doctor persuaded a former mistress, Madame de Pauw, to insure her life then feign illness, writing to him a letter detailing the imaginary malady and its cause, an equally imaginary fall on the stairs.

The insurance companies were persuaded, since her life was to be curtailed by this illness, to settle a yearly sum on her rather than pay a much larger capital sum on her death. The final deception was to get her to assign the policy to himself - much as Wainewright was to do.

Madame de Pauw died very soon afterwards from digitalis poisoning and the doctor's unseemly haste in claiming the cash aroused suspicion and sent him to the guillotine in 1864.

In London, through Eliza and Wainewright's ploys, some of the City's major insurance companies, the Eagle, the Palladium, the Pelican, the Hope and the Imperial, had been hoodwinked. The Globe and the Alliance had been suspicious enough to decline and the Provident had escaped providentially because the premium was not paid.

| Company | Sum assured | Duration |
|---|---|---|
| Imperial | £3,000 | 2 years |
| Palladium | £3,000 | 3 years |
| Pelican | £5,000 | 2 years |
| Hope | £2,000 | 2 years |
| Eagle | £3,000 | 2 years |
| | £16,000 | |

| Company | Sum proposed | |
|---|---|---|
| Provident | £2,000 | premium unpaid |
| Globe | £5,000 | declined |
| Alliance | £5,000 | declined |
| Eagle | £3,000 | declined addition to existing policy |
| | £18,000 | |

Had all the proposals been accepted, had all the insurance companies paid up, the scale of the fraud would have amounted to the colossal sum of £34,000, more than £3.5 million according to the Bank of England calculator

Perhaps if the Wainewrights tried to deceive just one insurance company they might have got away with it, though the sudden death of a healthy young woman would have been bound to raise questions.

To try to swindle eight London companies simultaneously was preposterous and showed not only excessive greed, but absolute recklessness - perhaps a legacy of that severe mental illness of 15 years previously.

The cost of the enterprise to Wainewright in premiums paid and stamp duty was £220. Unless something befell Helen, £201 would be needed to pay the premiums the following year.

Where had the money come from to pay these premiums, given that he already owed money to everyone from the village butcher to West End usurers? Again, it was begging and borrowing, for the rewards would be enormous.

## CHAPTER 8

## THE DEATH OF HELEN

The day of reckoning of December 21, 1830, Christmas Quarter Day, when Wainewright would have to pay back Sharpus the money lender his £610 in full or lose everything, was drawing now very close.

But there was no money to do so and other debtors were threatening; the Sheriff of Middlesex had put a bailiff into Linden House to try to assess how they could be paid, probably not knowing that Sharpus already had a lien on all the possessions in the house.

Then there were the tradesmen of Turnham Green, the grocer, the baker, the butcher the coal dealer, everyone except the candlemaker were pressing for the money that was owed to them, and they cut off the very extensive credit that they had extended to the young man-about-town.

On Sunday, December 12, Linden House was empty but for the bailiff. Wainewright, Eliza, two-year-old Griffiths, the sisters Abercromby and the two servants, Harriet Grattan and Sarah Handcocks had decamped from Turnham Green.

They had not gone far, only to central London, but at least it kept them away from the insistent demands for payments by the local tradesmen. They took up lodgings in the West End at number 12, Conduit Street, above the shop of Mr Nichol the tailor, a short walk across Regent Street from Great Marlborough Street and the earlier splendours.

The second part of the plan now came into operation. Until now the death of Helen might not even have been considered. A scheme to send her abroad might have worked. But it would have taken some little time to arrange, and there would have to be cash to set up the expedition on which Helen would have been 'mislaid'.

But the Wainewrights were without funds and time was running out too. There was only a week before Sharpus claimed his due, and then all would be lost – perhaps irretrievably.

On the morning of December 13 – a Monday – Eliza and the two sisters called on the Palladium Insurance Company. They wanted to assign the policy – that is transfer the benefit to someone else. But the company said they had no forms for such a transaction.

Then a crucial step had to be taken - Helen had to make a will. The same day, at lunchtime, Helen went by herself to Chancery Lane to the chambers in Tooks Court of a lawyer called Thomas Lys to sign the short document that was to cause such trouble in the Court of Chancery years later. She used her previous address in Sheen rather than Linden House or her new lodgings in Conduit Street.

> *This is the last will and testament of me Helen Francis Phoebe Abercromby of East Sheen in the County of Surrey Spinster. I assert that all my just debts and funeral and testamentary expenses shall be paid by my executor hereinafter named and subject thereto I give devise and bequeath all my real estate whatsoever and wheresoever whether*

*freehold copyhold or otherwise and all my personal estate whatsoever unto my Sister Madalina Abercromby of East Sheen aforesaid Spinster....... and I appoint Thomas Griffiths Wainewright of Turnham Green in the County of Middlesex Esquire sole Executor of this my last Will and Testament.*

She left and returned at 2pm to sign it "Helen ff.P. Abercromby". It was witnessed by Lys and two others from his chambers. One of them, Francis Slocombe, his clerk, was to say later that Helen had said that she was going abroad. Neither could have known that she had only a week to live.

Was Lys suspicious as to why a girl of 21 – by herself – should want to draw up her will? Helen asked him to make two copies. A couple of hours later she returned to sign them and took them away with her.

Lys was not the only lawyer that Helen saw that day. Another attorney, James Bird, knew Eliza by sight as he had known Mrs Abercromby, and knew that all she had had was an income from renting out a house in Mortlake.

That afternoon Eliza came to his office with a "little job" for him to do. While Helen stood by, he filled in, at Eliza's dictation, a form of assignment from the Hope Insurance Office transferring the benefit of Helen's £2,000 policy to Wainewright. It was an expensive business; Wainewright would have to pay consideration money of 19 guineas – Eliza replied that her husband would see to that.

The machinery for extricating Wainewright and Eliza from their financial plight was now almost in place.

After the unseemly departure from Turnham Green though there was some time to relax and for the sisters and Eliza to sample the delights of the town, which Wainewright knew so well.

That evening he took the family to the theatre. There were good bills at Drury Lane, the Royal Surrey and at Covent Garden. Indeed, at Drury Lane, they could see the famous Macready, a dinner companion of the past.

After the play there was supper at Conduit Street; once it might have been *foie gras* and champagne, tonight because of the financial situation it was oysters and beer, for oysters were not a luxury in 19th century London; Dickens refers to them several times as the diet of the poor.

The following morning there were more lawyers to see. Thomas Kirk had never met Helen before, but he was willing enough to do a simple task, like filling in a form of assignment. His job was made even easier as all the information necessary to transfer the Palladium policy of £3,000 to himself had been pencilled in.

Helen signed it. Again, the consideration money was not paid. The next port of call was Furnival's Inn, where Wainewright's uncle Robert (whose signature he had forged six years previously) was in practice as a solicitor.

He was one of the witnesses to another will made by Helen – her second in two days, this time in favour of Eliza, and of course Thomas Griffiths Wainewright, artist, of Linden House, Turnham Green. Robert could hardly have known that she had made a completely different will the day before.

The legal tangles were now all sorted out. The stage was now set. The visits to lawyers, which were to be described later by the Attorney-general as mysterious circumstances were over, so were the visits to insurance offices and the "misrepresentations", as the Attorney-general was to call them, of Eliza.

Helen Frances Phoebe Abercromby, spinster, aged 21, in perfect health, was now worth a huge sum of money dead, and through dubiously-obtained policies, two wills, made in two days and other legal machinations, Wainewright himself, and his family would collect – if she died within two years. But what chance was there of that?

More celebrations were called for. Helen and Madalina set out for the theatre for the second night in succession. There was "School for Scandal" at Drury Lane, "Cinderella" at Covent Garden and somewhat prophetically at the Royal Surrey a piece called "Van Diemen's Land".

What they saw we do not know, but when they did emerge from the theatre it had been raining. Through the damp streets they walked home to Conduit Street. Helen's feet were wet when they returned; she changed her shoes and stockings and then decided to go to bed.

She thought she might have caught a chill. But the others persuaded her to have some supper – once more it was to be oysters and porter. The meal, perhaps chosen deliberately was to be crucial. It was to be the last proper meal she ever ate, for that night she fell ill, and it was an illness from which she was never to recover.

A well-documented record of Helen's illness still exists. It comes from the evidence given by her doctor at the two civil court cases over the insurance policies, four years after her death, Dr Charles Locock gave his evidence in the two cases with some precision, despite the time that had elapsed since her death.

Perhaps he kept notes on the course of her illness. We do not know whether he was meticulous, but he certainly was eminent. He had a fashionable practice in Hanover Square, a few moments walk from Mr Nichol's lodgings. He specialised in 'ladies ailments', became obstetrician to Queen Victoria and was knighted for his services.

He was also in the public eye after examining John Ruskin's wife Effie six years after her marriage and pronouncing her *virgo intacta*. In Helen's case, his simple diagnosis and simpler remedies could do nothing to save her – and ironically two of his potions probably worsened her condition.

This was characteristic of the still-primitive state of medicine in the 19th century. The 1848 edition of *Buchan's Domestic Medicine*, for example, listed among the causes of disease "night air and wet feet" two things Helen had experienced.

The night after that second shellfish supper Helen had a bad headache, and was violently sick. And on the following morning, Wednesday, December 15, she still felt ill; it was a cold she thought, as she lay shivering on the settee. She managed to eat a little, then Wainewright sent out to the chemist for what was described rather ominously later as a "black dose".

This could have been one of two common 19th century remedies, either a 'black draught' a laxative of senna and Epsom salts, or the black drop', a painkilling mixture of morphine and acetic acid; Coleridge had become addicted to it.

Helen took it obediently, but it made no improvement, rather the opposite it seemed, for her condition worsened.

By the following morning, Thursday December 16, the family had decided that the doctor must be sent for. Dr Locock called in; he knew Helen quite well, as ironically again, he had certified her as healthy for one of her insurance policies.

She was sitting in her bedroom above the tailor's shop, complaining of a "great headache" shooting pains, a weight over her eyes, and partial blindness. Her pulse was very slow and laboured.

Locock gave her the first of his useless remedies, calomel, which was much prescribed for a variety of illnesses in the 19th century. It was, alas, highly toxic as it was inorganic mercury, which as the *Western Journal of Medicine* pointed out in 2000, can lead to stomach disorders, neurological symptoms such as tremors, and personality changes.

This toxic mixture was followed by senna as a laxative, as he was to testify later that he believed "a confused state of the bowels" leading to pressure on the brain was responsible for Helen's symptoms.

The following day he called at Conduit Street again. Helen's headache was no better so he decided to bleed her. This was a primitive procedure known as cupping, where the skin was cut open and a glass cup put over the wound. A syringe was used to extract air from the cup which had the effect of drawing out blood to release "impurities" from the body.

This procedure, it was said, relieved her headache for a time, but then her pulse became feverish. So to relieve the fever, she was given a dose of tartar emetic, which contains toxic antimony, for the purpose of making her vomit, which she did violently.

The doctor left when the spasms had subsided, and into her bedroom came Wainewright. As she lay there, weak from the bout of violent sickness, and four days from death, he had one last request to make of her, there was one more paper to sign.

It was another form of assignment, another transfer of one of her life policies, this time to Wainewright's solicitor John Atkinson. Helen signed over the £3,000 policy with the Eagle, obeying her brother-in-law almost to the last.

Atkinson, of course, had loaned a great deal of money to Wainewright over the years, since the man-about-town had first approached him for cash in 1826. Most of the money had been secured, so this latest venture could have been either to pay off an existing debt, or put in as security for yet another loan.

With either motive in mind, Wainewright must have been in a desperate hurry to get the document signed and he obviously had no compunction about making Helen do it on her sick-bed. Over the weekend she improved slightly.

On Sunday, when Dr Locock called again, the fever had gone down a little, and she had recovered her eyesight. For the first time since the illness began, she was able to eat something – a little broth. But the improvement did not last, during the night she was restless and became hysterical several times.

In the morning Locock prescribed a sedative, camphor tablets, and obviously puzzled by the course that the illness was taking, asked Eliza if she knew of anything that could be responsible for the continuing illness. Perhaps Eliza did know, but she told the doctor nothing that could help him.

Tuesday was December 21st, the Christmas Quarter Day, to which Wainewright would not have looked forward. For many weeks he had known that on this day the whole of the furniture and effects that remained in Linden House would fall forfeit to the moneylender Sharpus. There had been far too much money spent on high insurance premiums lately for there to be any left over to meet old debts.

Helen seemed much better again that Tuesday, Locock, in fact, thought that the improvement was considerable. But she was still easily excited and her pulse was still rapid. Locock decreed that she should be kept quiet, young Griffiths should not be allowed into her room.

If the improvement continued, he said, she could have meat the following day, which would be her first proper meal since that upsetting dish of oysters. Meanwhile, he advised her to continue with the camphor tablets, and as he left the house, he heard her asking for a cup of coffee.

The improvement, like the previous one, was not to last. At mid-day one of the two servants, Harriet Grattan, passing the door to Helen's room, saw Eliza bending over her. She was giving her something, a powder in jelly, the servant was to say later.

It was not a medicine that Dr Locock had prescribed, as he was to testify. A few minutes later leaving the sick-room Eliza declared that as Helen seemed so much better she and Wainewright would go out for a walk. As they went out of the house, Harriet sat at Helen's bedside. She lay quiet and rested.

Suddenly, at about two o'clock she became delirious. She heard a little boy in the room. "Is it Griffiths?" she asked, "he should not be in here." Sarah tried to calm her, there was no-one in the room except the two of them, she said. But Helen would not be pacified and burst into tears.

Then, just as suddenly as the delirium had begun, came a series of violent convulsions, her body thrashed and arched in the bed. Thoroughly alarmed, Sarah sent immediately for Dr Locock, who had been gone only just over two hours, and also sent for help to a nearby chemist's shop.

Edward Hanks the apothecary, was the first to arrive. He quickly gave Helen anti-spasmodic medicines, and the convulsions began to die away. A few minutes later Locock was there. He was to testify later: "she was in convulsions resembling those of a wound and was hysterical; she was sure that she would die." Gradually she became calmer saying to Locock: "Doctor, I was gone to Heaven, but you have brought me back to earth."

Harriet Grattan, who was also at the bedside remarked to Locock that Mrs Abercromby had died in convulsions the same way. Helen heard her whisper and cried out: "Yes my poor mother, oh my poor mother."

The convulsions had now gone completely, and the doctor and apothecary, convinced that the emergency was over, left the house. But no sooner had they gone than the convulsions began again, and this time even more violently.

Locock hurried back to Conduit Street for the third time that day, but he was too late. Helen had died clutching the hand of Harriet at four in the afternoon. There was nothing more that Locock could do now and as he left the house, he met Wainewright and Eliza returning from that stroll that had taken them out of the house, away from the agony of the last minutes of Helen's life.

Did they hear from Locock the news that they had been expecting or did it come as a great shock to them? To outward appearances, at least, Wainewright was surprised. Locock was to say later: "He appeared much shocked and astonished, as he had left her much better than she was the night before."

Then came a most important question: As the three stood in the street outside the Conduit Street lodgings, Wainewright asked: "What was the cause of her death? To this Locock replied sagely: "Mischief in the brain..."

To discover the cause of that mischief, he wanted to perform a post mortem. Wainewright assented readily. Locock asked whether Helen had had a love affair, perhaps suggesting that she had committed suicide.

Wainewright was quick to disabuse him of any such notion and Locock was to tell a court later under cross-examination that the family had behaved perfectly properly during Helen's ordeal. He was also one of the few people to be paid for his services immediately by Wainewright.

There was little time for grief, for later that afternoon there were more visitors at Conduit Street.

While Helen lay dead in the house, Sharpus the moneylender and his lawyer Cornwall called, demanding payment of that £610 for which they had waited for so long. And they were not to be put off this time. Wainewright again tried to postpone the reckoning, to talk Sharpus into giving him yet more time. But the two would have none of it. However, they could hardly wrangle about the money in a house of mourning, nor could Wainewright outline there to them the plan he had in mind. He would see them, he said, a little later.

That evening, with Helen dead but a few hours, Wainewright went to the crockery shop in Cockspur Street, carrying in his hand the two wills she had made, in perfect health, the previous week.

To Cornwall and Sharpus, he promised that their problems – and his – were over. He read them Helen's first will, bequeathing her formidable expectations of £16,000 to her sister Madalina. Then he read them the other, in favour of himself and Eliza. Cornwall, as a lawyer, was suspicious; why did a young girl have two wills – and why were they dated only one day apart? Wainewright dismissed this by saying that if one will failed, the other would do - so much for a last will and testament - and he also offered to assign to them Helen's policy in the Hope Company, now worth £2,000.

He had over-reached himself for Cornwall and Sharpus had smelled a rat, and they were not impressed by paper promises of great wealth to come. They would seek judgement on their warrant of attorney. Wainewright had lost the first battle.

The following day, the post-mortem began. Locock and the apothecary, Hanks, opened the skull of the dead girl. They found there what they believed to be the cause of death; there was a considerable quantity of water on the lower part of the brain, pressing on the spinal marrow.

The vesicles of the brain were loaded, so were some of the blood vessels, they noted. The water caused the convulsions and the convulsions caused the death. And why was there water on the brain? The two came up with the only solution they could think of. Oysters. They had produced similar effects on irritable constitutions before, and Helen's constitution was irritable because she had got her feet wet. It was all neat, logical, and explained everything.

The two also examined the stomach; there was nothing there that could possibly suggest foul play, said Hanks, and Locock agreed. The matter seemed closed. There was nothing left now but the burial.

However there was one last attempt to find out the truth. Thomas Graham, the surgeon, who had examined Helen earlier in the year was puzzled by the news of her death. While the family were living near him in Turnham Green he had never known her to have a day's illness. And indeed he himself had certified her to be perfectly fit.

Two days after Locock's post mortem he wrote to Wainewright asking if he could examine the stomach. Wainewright replied that other medical men had already done this; he was obviously reluctant to allow any more investigations into the death.

But Graham was not satisfied; he went to see Wainewright personally to insist on a further examination. Wainewright capitulated and there was a second post-mortem in which Graham took part with Locock and Hanks. Graham was given Helen's stomach in a bottle. He examined it minutely, but found only a slight inflammation, which could have been caused by the vomiting.

This "slight blush" as Locock was to call it, was not sufficient to justify any suspicions that Graham might have had; the word poisoning was never mentioned throughout this harrowing time. Though Helen's symptoms of arching and convulsions are now known as typical of strychnine poisoning, the medical men of the time would not have recognised it; it was recently-discovered and did not begin to figure in murder cases until much later in the 19th century.

According to W.C. Hazlitt's account of Wainewright's life, there was an inquest and the coroner's jury ascribed no blame to anyone for Helen's death. It seems that this might be a presumption on Hazlitt's part. Mr Gell, the coroner for the parish of St George's, Hanover Square, in which Conduit Street lay, held several inquests that December and January in the Turf Coffee House, Grosvenor Place, but not one on Helen.

The records of inquests in the parish of St. George in this period are kept in the Muniments Room at Westminster Abbey. The Keeper of the Muniments, Matthew Payne, has kindly searched the archive for any reference to Helen Abercromby and found nothing.

Given her age and the circumstances of her death this is surprising; today there would certainly be an inquest. But perhaps Dr Locock thought that after three medical interventions after her death had found nothing suspicious, there was no point in pursuing the case, besides and Christmas was a few days away.

There is also no reference to an inquest in any of the papers relating to the insurance claim which Wainewright was quick to make. Had an inquest jury found no suspicious circumstances, this would surely have been brought up in the insurance trials which were to follow.

Although Locock wrote a death certificate, it is not preserved in the national registry, as the statutory registration of births and deaths did not begin until 1837.

Helen's body lay in the house over Christmas. It must have been a strange time at Conduit Street, Madalina mourning the deaths of her mother and sister within a few months of each other and Wainewright and Eliza rejoicing quietly at the prospect of riches ahead.

On December 28th there was a brief burial service at St. George's, Hanover Square; the burial register records that Helen was one of three being interred that day by the Rector, Rev. Thomas Glen.

Where she lies now, in the St George's burial grounds at Mount Street, Bayswater Road or in St. George's Row, it is impossible to trace, as the burial books in the Westminster library are incomplete. But also most certainly there is now a block of buildings above her grave.

With the funeral over, and no suspicion of foul play attaching to Helen's death, Wainewright lost no time in telling the insurance companies of her demise.

The Eagle minute book recorded on Jan. 4 1831. Life assured died. Cause of death: "Fever with effusion at the base of the brain ending in convulsions".

When the claims were made, word soon spread around the insurance world that Helen had taken out policies with no fewer than five companies, that the Provident, too, would have been liable if the premium had been paid, and, worst of all, that two other companies had had the foresight to refuse the risk.

The directors of the Eagle met on January 4. Henry P. Smith, the company's actuary, was instructed by the board to enquire into Helen's death. At this stage, the companies thought that they had a case for refusing to pay on the grounds that there must have been foul play.

The Imperial Life's court of directors met on January 5, 1831 and decided to await further information before settling policy No. 1119. When they met again a week later, Dr Locock's death certificate was read to them, but in the meantime they had asked their own consulting physician, Dr Lidderdale, to investigate the death.

These Imperial papers, with Dr Lidderdale's report which could cast so much more light on Helen's end, are now lost and only the company's minute books survive in the Guildhall manuscripts room in the City of London.

The Imperial might have scented murder and fraud, but Wainewright was not to be accused at this stage of anything. No-one had mentioned the word poisoning. Helen's body had been examined by a surgeon, a physician and an apothecary who had found nothing amiss. His reasoning was that if the insurance companies would not pay voluntarily, they must be made to do so.

He decided to sue, even though a case in Chancery would cost money, and he had none. But lack of money was never an impediment to Wainewright.

He still had securities in the policies, which when the firms were forced to pay out, would make him a rich man.

Just before Helen's death, one of the policies had been assigned to the solicitor Atkinson, and it was to Atkinson's office in Basinghall Street that Wainewright went on January 27. He pointed out that the policy with the Palladium had been assigned to Atkinson to cover his existing debts. It was worth £3,000 and there was no reason to suppose that his case would be lost.

So if Atkinson would advance him another £1,000, all his other creditors could be paid off, and he would be able to start the suit in Chancery to get the cash from the Imperial which would go to Madalina, and with a successful ruling there the Palladium and Hope would have to pay out.

Atkinson, obviously a man of great forbearance, agreed. If the case became long and expensive, Linden House might stand as some sort of security.

With money in his hands at last, Wainewright paid off Sharpus in January 1831 with £610 and Atkinson's partner filed a bill in Chancery against the directors of the Imperial, on behalf of Helen's sister, the beneficiary of her will. Now this was an astute move, a judgement against one of the companies would stand as a precedent. They would all have to pay out then without further question. And what was more, the Imperial policy was not one in which Wainewright himself had a direct interest.

He had not assigned it to himself or anyone else and he was not the beneficiary, except ultimately under the second will – which he had no need to produce in court. As executor of Helen's first will he could claim an impartial interest in getting the money for the orphan Madalina.

But while the financial crisis was over for the time being, there was now domestic upheaval. Eliza left him, moving to the Kings Road in Chelsea, taking with her son Griffiths and sister Madalina. Why did she go? Did she leave, as one writer suggested later, in terror of being poisoned herself? Possibly. Although it was Eliza who taken her dead sister on a round of insurance companies and who had administered the final and fatal dose of medicine, she may well have feared that because of her complicity in Helen's death and the unexplained violent ends of her mother and Wainewright's uncle, she might be the next to go to preserve silence.

In the meantime Wainewright was without a wife, without friends. There was nothing more he could do until the Chancery case began, and there was the nagging apprehension that if the insurance companies delved too deeply into his affairs, the forgeries on the Bank of England could be brought to light. It was time to put himself out of reach of the authorities.

In an uncharacteristic gesture he paid off a debt of £200 to Madalina's suitor, the auctioneer Wheatley, on April 23. He had not real need to do so, for he was about to leave England – not to return until he had spent six years in exile.

# CHAPTER 9

# DEADLY TONICS

*"Strychnine is a grand tonic, Kemp, to take the flabbiness out of a man."*
H.G. Wells
*The Invisible Man*

Helen had died of the classic symptoms of strychnine poisoning, delirium, convulsions and the arching of the back. She had probably been weakened by other poisons before the fatal potion, powdered strychnine encased in sweet jelly to disguise its intensely bitter taste. The remedies prescribed by Dr Locock had hastened her end. So, perhaps, had a 'black dose' containing morphine.

How had it been possible to obtain the deadly strychnine? Because it was as easy to buy poisons as a loaf of bread in 19th century England. They were sold for a few pence by chemists, grocers, chandlers, agricultural merchants and other tradesmen.

The result was a virtual epidemic of arsenic poisoning, most of it accidental, as arsenic was used for many different purposes, not only to kill vermin, but taken as a tonic, used to improve the complexion, put on meat to kill flies and because of the Victorian passion for things bright green, arsenic derivatives such as Scheele Green were used in dyeing wallpaper, carpets, clothing and toys; touching or brushing against them exuded dust, poisoning their users.

But it was also used for much more sinister purposes. Tasteless white arsenic, not strychnine, was the poisoners' weapon of choice in Victorian times. To benefit from insurance policies, Mary Ann Cotton of County Durham poisoned her mother, three husbands, a lodger and most of her 15 children in the 1850s before justice very belatedly claimed her.[1] There were many proven and suspected cases of penniless women poisoning their children to claim money from burial clubs.

When Mary Miller was convicted of murdering several members of her family with poisoned cakes in 1847, the *Times* declared it "a woman's crime".

After an epidemic of poisonings in Essex villages, the paper was moved to ask:

*In other counties as well as Essex, wives are weary of their husbands... how is it then in Essex alone that inclination should become an act, and result in murder?*

In the 19th century 55% of women convicted of murdering their husbands used poison (*ibid*). Whereas men were likely to employ more violent means of homicide, the female murderer was depicted using stealth to drop poison into the victim's food or drink - then waiting calmly for the results. Needless to say this stereotype has been vigorously contested by those who have pointed put the large number of men convicted of the crime in the 19th century.

---
[1] Whorton, J C. *The Arsenic Century*. Oxford. 2010.

Not just arsenic was available. Among other deadly potions freely used in the 19th century for various purposes were cyanide, antimony, opium and, of course, the vegetable poison strychnine, though not common at the time of Helen's death. It was used to cure everything from paralysis to constipation, according to Dr. John Buckingham's book *Bitter Nemesis*.[2]

It was taken as a remedy against Spanish flu in the 1918 pandemic and promoted as a tonic well into the 20th century. It is alleged to be used covertly today to enhance sporting performance. It is on the World Anti-Doping Agency's list of banned substances.

Strychnine was discovered in France in 1818. It is a highly-toxic bitter alkaloid extracted from the seeds of the *strychnos nux-vomica* tree that grows in India and south-east Asia. France imposed strict controls on its use because of its danger, but in England there were no controls at all on the selling of poisons for many years, because of the typical reluctance of the British Government to interfere in the workings of the free market where profits could be made; arsenic manufacture was big business as it was used in so many different ways.

The fortunes of William Morris, for instance, the artist and print designer, who used arsenic extensively in his products, came mainly from his family's arsenic mines in Devon, which produced half the world's supply. He vigorously denied any connection between his products and poisoning.

---

[2.] Buckingham, J. *Bitter Nemesis: The Intimate History of Strychnine*. CRC Press, Boca Raton, U.S. 2007

Lobbying by arsenic manufacturers prevented any controls until, after a series of scandals, the Arsenic Act of 1851 required a register to be kept of who bought it, though anyone could still sell it.

It was not until the Pharmacy Act of 1868 that the sale of other deadly poisons was finally brought under control. The first part of the Act restricted the sale of strychnine, cyanide and ergot to chemists and druggists; sales could be made only to known persons and had to be entered into a Poisons Register.

Then there was the issue of how poisoning could be detected. Forensic methods were in their infancy in the early 19th century. The first attempt to codify existing knowledge was Christison's *Treaty on Poisons* in 1829. Between 1832 and 1836, James Marsh, a chemist at the Royal Arsenal at Woolwich discovered an infallible way of detecting arsenic in organic substances in the stomach. His test was followed by the Reinsch test in 1841.

Alkaloid poisons, like arsenic could now be identified, but vegetable poisons like strychnine could not as there was no significant test for them. This became clear in the Old Bailey insurance cases which followed Helen Abercromby's agonising end. It was not until 1883 that the Mandelin test was able to identify strychnine by using sulphuric acid to produce colour changes in material.

Helen died in 1830, only 12 years after strychnine had been discovered. According to the 19th century toxicologist, Dr Alfred Swaine Taylor, it was the first murder by strychnine perpetrated in Britain.

Strychnine does not begin to feature in poisoning trials in England until much later in the century. The two most famous cases in which it was used

The ease with which anyone could buy deadly poisons is exposed in this cartoon of 1846 by John Leech, a prolific contributor to the magazine Punch.

*Wellcome Images*

were those of medical serial killers. Dr Neil Cream, the Lambeth killer, was hanged in 1891 for the murders of several prostitutes and Dr William Palmer, of Rugeley, Staffordshire, who was executed in 1856 for murdering a friend, John Parsons Cook, over gambling debts, but had probably also killed members of his family.

The expert medical evidence of strychnine poisoning in the Palmer case was given by Dr Taylor of Guy's Hospital in London. His evidence caused great controversy because he had previously observed the effects of strychnine only on rabbits and no strychnine was found in Cook's body.

To answer his critics he produced a 150-page book after the trial, justifying his evidence.[3] The point he was trying to make was that there was still no reliable chemical test to detect strychnine so although the popular opinion, was as he put it, 'no poison found, no death from poison', other indicators such as symptoms could prove murder.

He cited in his defence the case of Helen Abercromby: "No-one who has considered the facts of this remarkable case can doubt that this young woman was poisoned by strychnia." Yet it had been attributed to 'cold and hysterical convulsions'.

Commenting on the use of strychnine in the Palmer case, the *Lancet* declared in 1855: "it is so

---

[3.] Taylor, A.S. *On poisoning by strychnia, with comments on the medical evidence at the trial of William Palmer for the murder of John Parsons Cook.* Longman, London. 1856. Taylor also pointed out that easily-obtainable vermin killers contained enough strychnine to kill humans. "They are openly sold by ignorant people to others still more ignorant".

speedily absorbed in the blood that in the course of an hour no chemical test at present known could detect it".

Helen died at four in the afternoon. The post-mortem did not begin until the following morning, long enough for any strychnine to disappear, even if there had been a reliable test to discover it.

The only evidence we have that strychnine was used to kill Helen, apart from examining the classic symptoms which led to her death, is hearsay - from a letter the actuary of the Eagle, Henry Smith, wrote to Bulwer Lytton the novelist several years afterwards. In it he said that Wainewright had confessed to using strychnine and morphine. The alleged confession was reported by Richard Thompson, who had been sent by Smith to monitor Wainewright's movements in France.

Smith went on:

> *There is no proof of the nature of the poison used, but the general medical opinion of the time pronounced it to be strychnine.*

There is no evidence that any doctor thought it was strychnine at the time; Smith was writing many years after the murder when more about strychnine was known.

If Helen was killed by this rare and deadly poison, how did the Wainewrights know about it? Carew Hazlitt suggested in his edition of Wainewright's essays that his knowledge might have come from Thomas de Quincey, his fellow contributor to the *London Magazine*, whose *Confessions of an English Opium Eater* in an 1821 edition, caused a sensation. He was fascinated by drugs and murder; Wainewright had met de Quincey at a dinner in November 1821 and had also invited him to his home.

In his 1827 essay *On Murder Considered as one of the Fine Arts* de Quincey wrote provocatively : "Fie on these dealers in poisons I say; can they not keep to the honest old way of cutting throats?"

A recent paper on homicide by strychnine read at a Leipzig symposium[4] detailed the appalling symptoms of the poisoning. Muscles begin to twitch 10 to 15 minutes after strychnine is taken; there is a state of apprehension followed by overwhelming fear. Major convulsions begin some 15 minutes later, triggered by an external stimulus. The back arches and limbs are extended, the jaw is tightly clamped and the diaphragm contracted. The patient may lose consciousness because they can't breathe, or through exhaustion caused by the convulsions; death follows.

One symptom not mentioned in the abstract is the characteristic *risus sardonicus,* the convulsive spasms of the muscles which make the face look as though it is grinning, though the patient is actually in desperate agony.

The muscular spasms caused by strychnine are similar to those experienced in tetanus, or lockjaw, when a wound is infected by bacteria, which is why Dr Locock thought that Helen's symptoms resembled those of a wound.

---

[4.] Benomam, F A. *Homicide by strychnine poisoning* in *Contributions to Forensic toxicology* . Molina Press, Leipzig. 1994.

According to Dr John Buckingham, another symptom universally reported by those who have taken strychnine is a feeling of impending death, something that Helen had referred to twice in her agonies.

After examining Helen's case he concludes that she was almost certainly killed with strychnine, but theorises that the Wainewrights must have subjected her to a weakening regime to make her eventual death more plausible. He suggests that tartar emetic was used for this, perhaps unaware that that this, and toxic calomel, were actually prescribed by Dr Locock to try to save Helen.

## CHAPTER 10

## A FLIGHT TO FRANCE

Criminals are often willing to change their names, but less ready to change their initials. This has led to much speculation about their unwillingness to lose their basic identities, but there is often a much simpler reason - the embarrassment which could be caused by monograms on baggage and clothing.

Thomas Griffiths Wainewright wanted to cover his tracks, so it was as Theodore G Williams that he presented himself at the French Consulate in London on April 23, 1831; the Theodore may have been a tribute to his artist friend Theodor (sic) Von Holst, who was to later support to his cause, even in exile in Van Diemen's Land.

On the other hand, he could have named himself after the Rev. Theodore Williams, the vicar of Hendon, whose enormous library had been sold by Wainewright's brother-in-law, the auctioneer Benjamin Wheatley in 1827.[1]

He requested a passport to travel to France; this was not a document like the present-day passport - more of a permit to travel in certain parts of France.

"Mr Williams" described himself as a *rentier*, bound for Paris via Calais. The clerk took his ten shillings and wrote down the details in the register:

---

[1] de Chantilly. *Under the Hammer*

| | | |
|---|---|---|
| *Age* | *36 ans* | *Front ord* |
| *Taille* | *5p 6* | *Nez long* |
| *Cheveaux* | *chat* | *Bouche moy* |
| *Sourcils* | *id* | *Menton rond* |
| *Yeux* | *bleus* | *Visage id* |

*Signes Particuliers -*

The description taken by convict authorities in Tasmania six years later differs slightly from this; Wainewright is half-an-inch shorter then - probably because a stoop had become more pronounced - and his eyes are said to be grey.

He was about to join a *galère* of English ne'er-do-wells in the French Channel ports, who had fled there for various reasons - to avoid the police, or like the heavily-indebted Beau Brummel in 1816, to outfox his creditors.

The start of Wainewright's self-imposed exile in France begins - in the legend - with a beautiful woman, and another killing. Walter Thornbury, in his *Old Stories Re-Told* an 1870 series of Victorian spine-chillers, sets the scene first in London, where Wainewright had won his way into the affections of the comely daughter of an old Army friend.

The widower - described as a Norfolk gentleman - lived in Bloomsbury. Wainewright is said to have been so fond of the daughter that he serenaded her with a guitar from the street, something he was also said to have done in London to another woman just before his arrest many years later.

When father and daughter, finding themselves short of money, decided to leave the country and settle in Boulogne, Wainewright followed them.

The financial problems grew so pressing that at Wainewright's insistence the Norfolk gentleman took out an insurance policy for £3,000 with the long-suffering Pelican company. On this he was able to raise a loan, but soon after the money arrived, and with only one premium paid, he took to his bed and died very suddenly. The symptoms: vomiting and coma.

Thornbury solves the mystery. "On the night he died, Wainewright insisted on making his friend's coffee and passed the poison into the sugar." It came, of course, from a poison ring - shades of Lucrezia Borgia - with a secret compartment full of *nux vomica*. The heartless poisoner took the money, and abandoned the orphan girl.

This is one of the oft-repeated and least attributable stories about Wainewright. "The whole tale would appear to be of the most doubtful authenticity", according to A G Allen in the 1894 book *Twelve Bad Men - Original Studies of Eminent Scoundrels by Various Hands*. It falls down because Allen checked with the Pelican, which had no record of such a policy, or of the Norfolk gentleman dying in Boulogne.

There could have been another insurance company, but the probability is that the story was an early Victorian accretion to the legend, based on no more than that Wainewright once stayed with such a couple in Boulogne. Another poisoning tale told of the death of a married woman Wainewright befriended in Calais. As Allen says, it is necessary, even in the case of the Borgias, to maintain an attitude of critical, if not incredulous reserve to such stories.

We do know that in Boulogne he was friendly with a lawyer, Pierre Hedouin, "deeply versed in music and the beaux arts" as he was to say later when he called him in aid in one of his petitions for mercy. Hedouin gave him letters of introduction to artistic friends in Paris.

Another intimate was Baron d'Ordre, Inspector of Water and Forests in the Pas de Calais and a noted *litterateur*. He wrote many books of prose and verse and his Swiss wife, Sophie, also published a volume of poems. Just the sort of company Wainewright would have sought.

Within a few weeks of his flight, probate of Helen's will was granted to Wainewright as her chief executor, which alarmed the Imperial to the extent that they referred the matter to the company chairman.

The record of Wainewright's six years in France is very patchy - except for one very well-documented month in 1835 when he was hounded by the British authorities. He seems to have spent most of the time destitute, painting and begging. In Paris, so it was said, he was arrested because of trouble over his passport and was found in possession of strychnine, which he could not explain; into prison he went for six months. Again these stories are not able to be confirmed.

He later claimed in his petition for mercy in Van Diemen's Land to have written and painted extensively while in France - a treatise on the beautiful in four volumes, an "Art Novel" in three volumes, one of which was already at the press.

Whatever his efforts, his former friends, who had dined in splendour at Linden House, began to receive begging letters from Calais and Paris. Barry Cornwall was one. He wrote later: "I received a letter from him, asking for a very small loan or gift in money, which I of course sent to him. The letter was in his usual fantastic style, referring to some pictures which I then had, particularly to my "dusk Giorgione" as he termed it.

But when he had to tell of his wretched state, his tone deepened. 'Sir, I starve,' he said, adding that he had been obliged to pawn his only shirt, in order to pay the postage on the letter. His letter exhibited great depression. He spoke of crowds of gay and careless people - gamblers and prodigals and others, all of whom passed him by - whilst he was "without a meal, without a single acquaintance and not knowing where he could apply with the smallest chance for help."

How he must have longed to join those prodigals, - he was, of course, one himself - to talk of his one-time artistic eminence in literary London, to mention his treasures, now long gone and to gallop once again in his chaise behind his horse Contributor.

Between 1831 and 1835 he drifted between Calais, Paris, Boulogne and St. Omer, painting and living on his wits. In Calais, he went into prison again; he had been living well at a hotel, but there was no money to pay the bill, so at the hotelier's suit back he went inside.

In 1834 he was living in St. Omer with a gentleman of means, a Mr Huntingdon, who had a house a mile outside the town on the Calais road. Despite his periods of destitution, he seemed to have had a knack of attaching himself to well-to-do patrons. He must have been there for some time because he dealt there with the correspondence relating to his claim against the insurance companies. A clerk to the solicitors acting for him came from London with some documents to be signed.

The clerk, a Mr Young, also took some news. Helen's sister, Madalina Rosa Hibernia Burdett Abercromby was now a wife. On May 19, 1832 she had married Benjamin Wheatley, the auctioneer who had who catalogued the library at Linden House before selling off the books. They were married by licence in St James' Piccadilly, a few steps from Wheatley's auction rooms.

It is notable that in the record of the marriage, one of the two witnesses is Eliza. Would Madalina have allowed her half-sister to take such a part in the ceremony if she was suspected her of complicity in the death of Helen?

While Eliza was living in poverty trying to bring up her young Griffiths, Madalina was faring rather better, living comfortably in Berners Street, off Oxford Street. In the summer of 1833 she commemorated her dead sister by naming her first child Madalina Helen. Her parents' name she remembered in the Christian names of her second child, Leonard Abercromby Wheatley, born the following year.

In Paris Wainewright had complained that no-one was taking any notice of him. Suddenly, this was no longer true. He became of intense interest to the Foreign Office in London, to the French Ministry of the Interior and to the Bank of England. The nemesis he had feared for so long had finally overtaken him - the forgeries had been discovered.

## CHAPTER 11

## A FRENCH FARCE

*"Bring him back to London by the next packet for Dover"*

Wainewright, living on his wits near Boulogne under the assumed name of Williams and painting to make ends meet, was unbeknown to him, about to be the central figure in a high-level Governmental farce involving the British Foreign Secretary the Duke of Wellington, the British Home Secretary, the Governor of the Bank of England, the French Minister of the Interior and various enraged insurance officials. The whole weight of officialdom was about to bear down on the hapless Wainewright - to absolutely no effect whatsoever.

The details which follow have never been published before. They have emerged from the archives of the Bank of England, mainly copies of letters between officials of the bank and its solicitors Freshfields, who trace their origins back to 1743 and are still the bank's solicitors, and from Foreign Office documents in the National Archives.

By 1835, Wainewright's audacious forgeries, draining the family trust fund from the Bank of England, had remained undetected for more than ten years. They might well have done so for even longer but for the curiosity of Wainewright's solicitor cousin, Edward Foss, the trustee in the marriage settlement and the bequest of old Dr Griffiths.

Foss knew that Wainewright was in France. Was he still receiving the dividends from the annuities? On January 15, 1835, Foss went to the Bank of England. The reply to his question was short: "There is no such stock." Foss insisted, the Bank officials argued politely, but gradually it began to dawn on them that they had been duped, and what was more they were liable for the loss of £5,250 - some £600,000 in present day terms, according to Bank of England's inflation calculator.

Foss returned to his office in Essex Street and wrote formally to the Chief Accountant demanding that the stock be replaced. He added: "Mr Robert Wainewright (*who was of course Wainewright's uncle*) and I will be ready to give the Bank every information and assistance in our power in tracing the guilty parties."(sic)

The next day at noon both men were at the Bank. They were seen by the Chief Accountant, William Smedley, who showed them the two forged documents which had made Wainewright a present of his son's inheritance. Another was found, but this was a minor matter, a power of attorney made out in 1825 to Wainewright's broker Mackintosh, to enable him to receive some forgotten dividends.

The two trustees pored over the signatures on the other documents. "They were generally very well executed", admitted Foss in an unwilling tribute to Wainewright's penmanship. "With some variations as to two of them which would have satisfied their supposed writers. But the names and the descriptions of the witnesses, which appeared to be wholly fictitious, were direct evidence of the forgery."

In the first document there was no such George Hughes of Grays Inn Lane, copying clerk, nor William Sturges of City Road, who purported to be clerk to Robert Wainewright. In the second, Thomas Stone, of Cary (sic) Street, clerk to Edward Eyre of Grays Inn, did not exist

The hunt was on. Both men crossed the road to the Mansion House to swear out a deposition before the Lord Mayor; things were beginning to move quickly.

The Governor of the Bank of England and his deputy, outraged that they had been swindled, wrote to the Home Secretary, Henry Goulborn:

> As this is a fraud of so very serious a nature affecting the integrity of the National Debt we venture to request the assistance of the British Government with that of France to procure the apprehension of Wainewright and that the necessary communications may be made to the Consuls at Calais and Boulogne to procure such assistance as may be required by the officer who will be despatched from thence for the purpose.

Victorian authors who wrote about Wainewright claimed that the Bow Street Runners, John and Daniel Forrester, were sent to France to pursue him, but they were not from the Runners, an anachronism soon to be absorbed into the Metropolitan force, founded by Sir Robert Peel six years earlier. The Forresters[1] belonged to the City of London Day Police - the forerunners of the City police. They were charged with bringing him back because the offences had taken place within the City of London itself rather than within the jurisdiction of the Met, and only one of them was sent.

On January 17, 1835, Daniel Forrester received his instructions: "You will proceed to Boulogne by the first opportunity... Mr Thompson who accompanies you will know the person and the residence of the culprit. There can be no difficulty in finding or tracing the culprit. Bring him back to London by the next packet for Dover."

Two major strands in Wainewright's undoing were now beginning to come together. For Richard Thompson, who played the dominant role in the farce to come, was not a Bank or police employee. He was working for the Eagle Insurance company, either directly for the Eagle's formidable actuary Henry Smith, or for Le Blanc, Oliver and Cook, the Eagle's solicitors.

The Eagle, and all the other insurance companies, had a vested interest in knowing Wainewright's whereabouts and motives, as they were about to be sued for monies due on Helen's death, and it seems likely that one of Thompson's tasks had been to

---

[1.] The Forresters' names appear as police constables in the Hall Keeper's Police Disbursements Book at Guildhall, with Daniel marked absent for the time he was in France. John continued to report for duty in the City, though a year later he was in France too, trying to arrest three leather-sellers on a charge of forgery. A Home Office recommendation to the Foreign Office described him as "a very intelligent officer".

keep an eye on Wainewright until the case against the Eagle came to court.

It is clear in one of his letters relating to Wainewright's time in France that one or more of his former servants had been sent there to identify him to his pursuers. He was known, said Thompson, as "Painter" Williams and lived with Mr Huntingdon. He had dark moustaches, sometimes large, sometimes small. Then, a surprising revelation: "He disguises very much; in general he wears little hair, but sometimes wears a curly wig."

As Thompson and Forrester jolted down to Dover. A letter went the same night to the British Consul at Boulogne, William Hamilton. It asked him to give the two men every assistance.

Hamilton, who from the start had grave doubts about their mission, already knew about Wainewright: it was his job to do so, for Boulogne at that time was a haven for renegade Britons and those who wished to conceal certain matters, such as the birth of illegitimate children. Charles Dickens kept his mistress the actress Ellen Ternan and her mother there for some time, Claire Tomalin, in her biography of Dickens, suggests that she gave birth in France to a son who died in infancy.

While Dieppe further down the coast attracted a more refined English colony, Boulogne and Calais were a refuge for debtors and those who had crossed the law. The French ferry ports were easily reached and, most important, there was no treaty of extradition between the countries, a fact which was signally overlooked by Freshfields, the British Government and everyone else involved.

In fact, the very day that the fraud was being discovered in London, the British Chargè d'Affaires in Paris, Arthur Aston, was writing a private note to the Foreign Secretary bemoaning the fact that two British police officers, already in France, were unable to arrest and bring home three wanted men. It was pretty clear that their objectives would not be attained and he had recommended them to return to England. "The laws of France do not permit the Agent of a Sovereign Government to arrest an individual on French territory".

On January 19, Thompson sent his first report from Hughes's Royal Hotel to Freshfields at New Bank Buildings. The news was not good: they would not be coming back on the next packet after all. Hamilton had told them that what they wanted to do was "utterly impossible". The local police chief and the Mayor had said they could do nothing without a command from the French Ministry of the Interior.

Thompson was shocked: "They think nothing of his (Wainewright's) going under an assumed name or being without a passport as there are hundreds of others in a similar situation." He outlined the difficulties he and Forrester were facing by giving an example - Ledbitter, the Bow Street Runner, had been there for three weeks trying to arrest the Rev. Henry Snell, treasurer of the St. Albans Savings Bank, who had made off to the continent with all the funds and was busy spending them.

At New Bank Buildings precedents were consulted. To Hamilton were sent details of Samuel Hall, convicted in London for stealing from his employer in Calais. Freshfields hoped the Boulogne authorities would take the hint and allowed Forrester to arrest Wainewright. But Hamilton wrote back to say they could not be budged.

Despite Aston's letter to the Foreign Secretary; a letter arrived at British Embassy in Paris instructing Aston to press the French Government for extradition. The initiative had moved into diplomatic channels, but little happened.

Thompson reported "with unfeigned regret" on January 28 that no word had been received from the Embassy. "I could go there", he suggested, "and push things on a bit." Hamilton, knowing that diplomacy could not be jerked into action, persuaded him not to go. There would be a telegraph from Paris at any hour; if Thompson went there he would be unable to formally identify Wainewright at his arrest in Boulogne. The delay was inevitable - it was the first case of its kind since the Revolution.

On January 30 the Foreign Office made more representations to the French. Still no action and Thompson was getting beside himself. Hamilton wrote: "He is most anxious to get the business settled, but this I regret to say, does not depend upon him, and from the knowledge I have of matters of this nature, it requires time."

Two days later Thompson thought he saw a way out of the impasse. "We may soon, very soon, be in a situation to return, crowning our mission." But it was a false hope; four days later he reported that there was still no word from Paris; meanwhile a strict watch was being kept on Wainewright.

Things were moving in Paris, but very slowly. The Charge d'Affaires, Arthur Aston, wrote again to the

Ministry of the Interior, the Comte de Rigny, asking for permission for Forrester to make the arrest:

> *Paris 3 February 1835*
> *Monsieur le Comte,*
> *I have received instructions from His Majesty's Government, to address to Your Excellency another representation respecting the individual named Wainewright who is charged with the commission of an extensive fraud upon the Bank of England, the details of which I had the honour to submit to Your Excellency in my Note of the 21st.*
> *An English Police Officer is now waiting at Boulogne (at or near which place Mr Wainewright is residing) in order to take into custody that individual so soon as the necessary authority be granted by the French Government, and it is of importance for the furtherance of the ends of public Justice that the decision of the French Government as to the mode of attaining that object be made known with as little delay as possible.*
> *Referring Your Excellency for further particulars to the note before mentioned I have only to add that the case is one in which His Majesty's Government take a deep interest.*

The reply came the following day: the Minister of the Interior regretted - but there was nothing he could do; no treaty of extradition existed between the two countries. Then, a curious passage:

> *However, and to answer as much as lies with him to the wish of the British Government, the*

*Minister of the Interior has given the order to the competent authorities in the Department where Mr Wainewright lives to make a search of his house and seize sums of money which they may find there. I will certainly let you know the result of this action, which has previously, on two more or less similar occasions, been successful.*

The Minister seems to have misunderstood; Wainewright was not sitting on piles of golden sovereigns stolen from the Bank, but living in some penury. Although Aston had stirred the French into action, he did not imagine anything would result from the search. Writing the following day to the Foreign Secretary, the Duke of Wellington, he did not even mention it, reporting only that extradition was impossible. The case seemed closed.

In the meantime, Thompson goaded beyond endurance by the delay, hired a carriage and clattered off to Paris "to push things on a bit". He was, of course, unsuccessful and to add to his misfortune, the carriage overturned on the way back to Boulogne, delaying him for six hours. The fruitless expedition cost him £25 2s, which included "post-horses, postillions and repairs to carriage."

Now he had a new idea – if there were no official treaty of extradition, perhaps an unofficial exchange might be arranged. The word had come from Paris that Wainewright's house was to be searched; if he could be arrested by the French for some breach of their own laws, there was a chance that the whole affair might speedily be settled by an exchange with a Frenchman in trouble in Britain. Success was in sight again.

He wrote to Freshfields: "The authorities here were willing, if they could, to punish him for any offence committed against the laws here, and it was arranged that our immediate search of his house and papers and our interrogation of himself should directly take place." It took two days to arrange, but then on February 14$^{th}$ a small party arrived at Wainewright's front door at eight in the morning – the Mayor, the Juge de Paix, Thompson, Forrester and the gendarmerie.

Thompson took careful note of the proceedings: "After first stating that his name was Williams, he corrected himself and said his name was Wainewright, alleging as a reason that he had melted his fortune, and wished to pass the remainder of his days unknown to his relations." Then he admitted he'd entered the country under a false name, with a French passport, but he did not have it with him.

In fact, he had become parted from it at Calais the day he had landed in France. The document, said Wainewright, was at Rignolles Hotel; he had never had it back. This may have been because he left without paying, a well-known gambit of his.

The interrogation over, Thompson searched through Wainewright's papers, but, disappointingly, nothing of importance relating to the fraud was found.

However, there was some evidence; he had entered the country with a false passport. Thompson persuaded the local officials to leave two gendarmes guarding Wainewright while the rest of them went off to consult the Juge d'Instruction and the Procureur. Their advice was to send to Calais for the passport; if it were false, then a three-month prison sentence lay ahead.

As an additional safeguard, Thompson wrote to Freshfields asking them for a copy of the entry in the Register of the French Consulate in London. This was sent post-haste.

On February 16$^{th}$, he wrote triumphantly to Freshfields: Wainewright had been arrested, examined by the Juge d'Instruction and committed to take his trial before the Correctional Tribunal.

Now came the dubious part: "This course has been pursued to enable you to exert your influence with the Duke of Wellington to cause him to be delivered up, or to endeavour to exchange him for any criminal (French) in England that the French Government may request to be delivered up in his place, of which, we are informed, there are two or three. His trial will be purposely delayed to the extent of 15 days to enable this object to be carried into effect."

The following afternoon, Thompson and Forrester left for home. Wainewright was behind bars, their job was almost done. But no sooner had they arrived in London than appalling news arrived from Hamilton in Boulogne. Wainewright had been freed – and the judge who had committed him there was in trouble.

Wainewright's counsel had complained that he was being held illegally – because the Statute of Limitations for passport offences was only three years, and Wainewright had obtained his four years before.

"His counsel", reported Hamilton, "pretends that the 'right of refuge' has been most shamefully violated, he will not leave the matter there, which does not little alarm the judge." As well it might if he had acted unconstitutionally.

The prisoner exchange plan had collapsed There was little Hamilton could do, but he didn't think Wainewright would leave Boulogne because he had no money and no passport. The Bank received the news with "much surprise." They asked Hamilton to watch him closely – "he will, have course, decamp if he can."

In London the Foreign Office, presumably themselves under pressure from the Bank and the Home Office, badgered Aston constantly to intervene with the French Government. In a series of notes, Aston played diplomatic ping-pong with the French Minister of the Interior, de Rigny, in a game he could not win.

On February 20 he reported to London: "The French Government will not be induced to take any further steps in this matter". He must have tired of telling them the same thing.

Disappointed at seeing the swindler slip out of their grasp, the Bank wrote peevishly to the Foreign Office to ask what further could be done. "If it is understood that persons in France are safe from the pursuits of justice, it will be useless in future for the Bank to incur the expense of sending persons thither in pursuit of them."

They must have just had the expense claims from Forrester and Thompson. Thompson got £103 9s 6d, including the cost of his abortive Paris trip, and paying £5 to two policemen to watch Wainewright's house for 25 days. Forrester claimed £59 0s 6d for his 34 fruitless days.

For him it was a profitable trip; Freshfields were paying him 15s a day whereas the City Police paid only £1 10s a week. Meanwhile, in Boulogne, the

Consul kept up a watch – at a cost of two francs a day.

Early in March, Wainewright applied for a passport – it is so described but would have been a permit to travel, to go to Paris; it was refused. On the 17th, Hamilton reported: "He seldom or ever comes into town. It would appear that he does not like the idea of leaving without a passport."

The Foreign Office pressed on: rather than Wainewright being sent home, if the French Government just expelled him he might return anyway.

Aston replied wearily on March 23, 1835: "As long as he does not transgress the laws of France he cannot be compelled to leave". They could also not prevent him "embarking on any vessel bound elsewhere".

By the end of March, it was obvious that nothing more could be done. The Foreign Office said so, as well as Hamilton. The Bank ordered the watch to be called off, but if Wainewright left Boulogne they still wanted to be told.

In Paris, Aston returned to more congenial diplomatic occupations, reporting conversations with King Louis Phillippe about the difficulty of finding a new husband for the newly-widowed Queen of Portugal.

What Wainewright himself thought of this fiasco is not known, but it must have amused him greatly to see the mighty Bank of England fumbling the case so badly. But it was also a warning that his forgeries had finally been discovered and that he could no longer safely return to England.

It was a warning that he did not heed.

## CHAPTER 12

## - INTERLUDE -
## THE RED BARN FANDANGO

"Maria Marten" – the story of the Murder in the Red Barn – was the great Victorian melodrama. It is still performed in repertory theatres today, more than 170 years after William Corder, the Suffolk farmer's son, was hanged for the killing of his mistress, Maria. Whether he was guilty or not there is now doubt. Very few people ever knew what really happened in the barn in the village of Polstead that May afternoon in 1827; one of them was alleged to be Wainewright.

What follows here is a lurid tale about the murder told in *The Red Barn Mystery,* a non-fiction book published in 1967 by one Donald McCormick, a *Sunday Times* journalist and colleague of Ian Fleming. He died in 1998 after turning out 50 or so books concerned with murder and espionage, some under the pseudonym Richard Deacon. Much of his output relied on 'secret diaries' and letters which have yet to be discovered by anyone else.

The tale is included here because it combines real facts about the murder with quotes from letters purporting to be written by Wainewright and extracts from diaries and other material linking him to the killer.

So to begin: Among Wainewright's neighbours in Great Marlborough Street, claimed Mc Cormick, was a dark, devious beauty who called herself Hannah

Fandango (sic), the daughter of an English sea captain and a Creole mother. After a good education, she had gone on the stage, become a dancer, then the mistress of a series of Guards officers.

But her conduct was so outrageous that she was ousted from military society to become a prostitute and procuress for a brothel-keeper, Despite her life, she had avoided " the ravages of her trade" and remained beautiful; it was claimed that Wainewright painted her often.(No paintings have ever been recorded let alone found).

There was another side to her life. Although living in some splendour in London, she stayed much of the time in the country, where she lived in a hut and told fortunes. The hut was within a mile of Polstead and it was there that she met William Corder, who soon became her lover.

When he was exiled by his father after a series of petty frauds, it was to Hannah that he turned. He was then about 22, thin, stooping and near-sighted; well-read but feckless. His sight was too bad for him to enter the Merchant Navy, his first objective as a career. He thought of newspapers, but decided: "From what I have seen, I am not sure that I have the stomach for it. Something of a literary nature would be more congenial."

Hannah knew just the man to help him; she gave him a letter of introduction to Wainewright and the two became close, Wainewright saying: "I found him a fascinating character in a dreary world. He would often call around to see me and I would be regaled by an account of his amorous adventure."

Many years later, an actress name Caroline Palmer, unconvinced of Corder's guilt, is said to have written to Wainewright in Van Diemen's Land and asked how well he had known him. Wainewright is said to have replied:

*I have in my time supped with the Olympians and danced with the Satyrs and Fauns and who shall say whether I learned more from the former than the latter? Not I. William Corder I recall as a kind of Satyr who only came to light when touched by love, a sentiment which he exuded as the flowers exhale sad perfume from their buds. Love for him was a kind of sad lament, like that of Moschus for Bion.*

*He came to me from the Suffolk countryside, a stooping youth with Napoleonic gestures and a sense of drama. I think he wanted to dramatise himself. He wanted to write, but he was, shall we say, more a Satyr than a satirist, fonder of words than they were of him, and if the written word is not enamoured enough of the writer to dance a minuet across his pregnant gaze, he will be hard put to know what to put on paper.*

*Yes, Corder went with me once to Brittany, and he also came with me to Boulogne with Hannah and I seem to remember they had a terrible quarrel that ended their always tempestuous relationship. Yet it was Hannah who had the violent temperament and Corder who was the cooing dove.....*

It continues in much the same vein...

*On the subject of forgery I may not be entirely guiltless of having implanted some ideas in*

*Corder's mind. He often complained about being kept short of funds by his father and I recall telling him that such treatment was foolish because it encouraged forgery and I explained how very easy it was to forge cheques and remain undetected – at least undetected for a considerable period.*

In 1827, Wainewright is said to have suggested that Corder set himself up as a private tutor in some little place like Turnham Green or Ealing "close to London but not as expensive as being in the heart of the Metropolis." The same year, having begun a relationship with Maria Marten, the mole-catcher's daughter, and still in the toils of Hannah, Corder advertised for a wife in the *Morning Herald*, one that "had the power of some property."

By remarkable chance, one of the 99 replies came from the girl on whom he had already set his heart – the quiet and wistful Mary Moore. Wainewright chose their home in Ealing Lane, which they made into a small school. The two families visited each other, Wainewright noting; "They seemed to be living an idyllic existence." The idyll was soon to be shattered. Corder grew uneasy; Wainewright suspected he was being blackmailed by Hannah. Then, the decomposing body of Maria Marten was found under the floor of the Red Barn.

Maria had become Corder's mistress in 1826. He had returned home after one of his tempestuous quarrels with Hannah, forsaking one wanton for another. Maria already had two illegitimate children – one of them by William's brother. By the late summer, she was pregnant again. The child

– acknowledged by Corder – was born sickly and died. Together, the two of them buried the body in a small box in a field.

Shortly afterwards, the Marten family were told there was to be a wedding – but Maria had disappeared. Eleven months later, her stepmother had a "dream". It gave, she claimed, precise details of where Maria's body was buried. Her father dug in the Red Barn, and there was the corpse.

Corder was arrested and charged with murdering Maria – and also accused of forging a cheque for £93 on an Essex bank. The forgery he admitted, but not killing Maria.

In a confession before he was hanged at Bury St Edmund's jail he admitted shooting her after a quarrel about the burial of the child. But he swore he had no knowledge of the stab wounds in her neck and side – the injuries more responsible for her death than the shot wounds.

The purported Wainewright went on: "In Tasmania, I came across an acquaintance of Corder's, a rascally, if picturesque convict who had been sent to Van Diemen's Land, known by the remarkable name of "Beauty" Smith . He told me that Corder had suffered a grave miscarriage of justice."

After Corder's execution, his sister – convinced of his innocence – is claimed to have came across old diaries which told of his life in London and of his friendship with Wainewright. "But I destroyed the diaries all the same, as I did not wish anyone should find them who, being of a malicious turn of mind, might try to link William with the convict Wainewright and so further besmirch his name."

After *The Red Barn Mystery* was published I contacted McCormick and asked for details of his sources, specifically to do with Caroline Palmer and the destroyed diaries. He replied very courteously: "I cannot help you very much but you are at liberty to quote from my book. What I included was compiled entirely from notes taken from a third party". (Unnamed)

In this tangled tale we have destroyed diaries, letters unseen by any other researcher of Wainewright's life, an unnamed supplier of details and paintings of 'Hannah Fandango' yet to be discovered...

The deceased McCormick's Wikipedia entry details his literary output and adds: "Many of these books included doubtful elements: extremely valuable sources that no-one else had ever heard of and that never saw the light of day after publication".

A 2014 book on the Mrs Thatcher's favourite economist, Friedrich Hayek, contains for reasons which need not detain us, "an assessment by a number of academics and specialists of what has been termed McCormick's 'fraudulent career', which includes evidence supplied by his personal papers".[1]

He is referred to elsewhere as a 'fantasy historian'. The noted historian A J P Taylor said of one of Mc Cormick's non-fiction books on spying: "No more preposterous book has ever been written". As far as Wainewright' tale is concerned, the *Red Barn* runs it close.

For what it is worth, Mc Cormick, in his letter to me, wrote that he thought that Wainewright's guilt in the poisonings was not proved.

---

[1] Leeson, R (ed) Hayek: *A Collaborative Biography Part III, Fraud, Fascism and Free Market Religion.* Palgrave Macmillan, 2014.

## CHAPTER 13

## "THE FATAL CUP"

In June 1835 Wainewright was still abroad, a hunted fugitive since the forgeries had been discovered, and after chronic delays the legal machinery clanked into action to try to resolve his claim against the Imperial insurance company, brought by his solicitor Atkinson, who had a major financial interest of his own in it.

This was a civil action; no criminal charges had resulted from Helen's highly-suspicious death despite the doubts of the insurance companies.

While it was only the Imperial that had been brought to court, all the other companies with which Helen's life had been insured had a major financial stake in seeing that the case was thrown out, as a verdict in Wainewright's favour would set a precedent by which all they would all have to pay out.

Wainewright had no money to pay his legal team, but five years previously he had assigned one of the policies to Atkinson, so a successful verdict would mean that Wainewright's debts to him would be paid off and his court costs met.

Wainewright was a nominal plaintiff, he would have had nothing to do with the case now he was in exile; it was brought by Madalina's lawyers as Helen's will left everything to her. But he was still her executor and after her death he had had to swear an oath to administer her estate before the will could be proved.

129

It was approved on May 21, 1831 before he fled to France, in Doctors' Commons – the College of Advocates and Doctors of Law, near St Paul's Cathedral in London, described by Dickens as... "the place where they grant marriage-licenses to love-sick couples, and divorces to unfaithful ones; register the wills of people who have any property to leave, and punish hasty gentlemen who call ladies by unpleasant names".

He was suing the Imperial as the executor of Helen's estate, so a successful outcome against the Imperial would benefit Madelina by £3,000 but render him nothing. However there were other policies which had been assigned to him and if the Imperial had to pay up the precedent would have been set for the others to be forced to do so too.

Much of the evidence that was given has already been used to reconstruct the story of the policies and of Helen's illness. What is of interest is the trial before a special jury and the submissions.

There was an imposing and expensive array of legal talent that morning of June 29, 1835, before Lord Abinger and a special jury in the Court of Exchequer to hear the case of Wainewright v Bland and others – these being three directors of the Imperial, he suing them. The Court of Exchequer dealt with civil cases involving financial matters and was to be merged with Chancery court a few years later.

For the plaintiff, Wainewright, appeared Mr Erle, Sir William Follett and Mr Henderson, a trio of expensive lawyers. Atkinson must have fairly confident about winning the case. On behalf of the

Imperial were the Attorney-general, Sir Frederick Pollock, Mr Thesiger and Mr Robinson.

The appearance of the Attorney-general showed the concern felt by the insurance companies. Although this was not a criminal trial, there was a convention that the Attorney-general always prosecuted in poisoning cases, a tradition that persisted until the famous trial of John Bodkin Adams, the Eastbourne doctor cleared at the Old Bailey in 1957 of doing away with his elderly lady patients.

Mr Erle opened the case for Wainewright, who, he said, who had no interest in the case except as the executor of the will of Helen Abercromby. The real party interested was Madalina, to whom Helen had left everything and Wainewright was bringing the action as Helen's executor and trustee. No mention was made at this stage of the other will, the one in which everything was left to Wainewright and his wife, or indeed of the all other policies.

He continued his opening statement with a brief recital of the facts of Helen's death and went on to point out that the death was natural. At a post-mortem, a doctor and an apothecary had come to the conclusion that that the cause of her death was fluid pressing on the base of the spinal marrow of the brain.

Mr Erle probably had an intimation that the Attorney-general would make the issue of poisoning a major plank of the Imperial's defence case, so he attempted to forestall it by saying that there was no sign of any poison. Her doctor, Dr Locock, had said there was nothing in the stomach which could be a cause of death.

Witnesses were called; the actuary of the Imperial; the Wainewright's servants Sarah Handcocks and Harriet Grattan and Mrs Nichol the landlady at No 12 Conduit Street, who testified that when she let the rooms early that December, Helen was "a remarkably healthy blooming young woman." All were cross-examined but there was no indication of which way the case was going.

Then came Dr Locock; he gave his views on Helen's illness and in cross--examination was forced to admit that the majority of vegetable poisons left no trace; strychnine, of course is a vegetable poison, but the word was not mentioned.

The Attorney-general opened for the Imperial by planting suggestions in the jury's mind. He did not know he said, what their opinion would be - whether Helen had come to her death by the visitation of God or by poison, but whatever their opinion, Wainewright had no right to claim this money.

The meaning was clear. Wainewright, said Sir Frederick, was entirely destitute of all pecuniary resources, except those he had raised by a loan when he began insuring Helen's life. The policies had been issued under mysterious circumstances. It was clear that she was a mere puppet of Wainewright's in the ten days before her death.

Sir Frederick, having introduced the issue of poisoning as a possibility now came to it directly: Helen's symptoms, though consistent with nature were not inconsistent with poison. It was only mineral poison (rather than vegetable) which could be detected in the stomach. Was it oysters or medicine that had caused her death?

She was much better when Dr Locock saw her at 11am on the Tuesday. He returned at two, but in the interim, Mrs Wainewright administered some powder to her which the doctor did not prescribe. The servant had sworn to it and Dr Locock had testified that the powder was nothing to do with him.

"That," declared the Attorney-general dramatically, "was the fatal cup." Shortly after Helen screamed and continued in convulsions to her death.

He continued disingenuously that he did not mean to say that Mrs Wainewright *knew* that she had administered the poison, but the jury might have read of the case of Miss Bland, who poisoned her father. When he was writhing in agony she had said: 'I will administer a dose to you that will mitigate your pain' and at the same time administered poison. Such was the case of Mrs Wainewright, but he hoped she had done it unconsciously.

The Attorney-general was making it quite plain that despite a lack of medical evidence of poisoning, there was no doubt that murder had been committed. But he had over-reached himself; citing the 'fatal cup' and the case of poor Miss Bland – no relation to the Imperial director who was being sued – and associating her with the Wainewrights was a step too far.

He had just said that as Helen was recovering on the day of her death, and the doctor had left, "Mrs Wainewright administered a medicine..." when the judge stopped him in his tracks. The jury were not there to try that issue, such evidence was not admissible as it might prejudice their decision, which, of course, had been Sir Frederick's strategy all along. The judge continued that if the object were to prove a charge of murder, more relevant evidence should be given.

So the poisoning issue was ruled out - a decision that infuriated the insurance companies; one of them was to describe it later as interfering in the course of justice. But there was a complete lack of forensic evidence to show that Helen had been poisoned, because the science was not there to enable it.

Rebuked, Sir Frederick moved to a new line of attack, relying on a statute that in every policy of insurance the name of the person for whose use and benefit it was effected had to be mentioned. In this case, the benefit was for Wainewright, even though Helen's name was on the documents.

He added another line to the Imperial's defence: Helen and the Wainewrights had been guilty of misrepresentation at all the offices, concealing the fact that she had made other insurances, therefore the Imperial policy was void. She had given differing reasons for the insurance and some of the banknotes used to pay the premium had been traced back to Wainewright.

Wainewright's counsel, Mr Erle, had a complete answer; there was no fraud or misrepresentation. The Imperial knew that Helen had taken out another policy therefore, having taken the premium they were obliged to fulfil the contract. Even if Helen had been murdered, it was no defence, though the poisoning issue had been raised only to prejudice the jury. The examination and evidence of Dr Locock was a complete answer to the insinuation.

Lord Abinger summed up weightily. There was a great deal of mystery about the transaction and many of the circumstances were calculated to evoke suspicion He thought he'd heard too much about the possibility of murder.

For even if Wainewright had killed Helen, the Imperial would still have to pay because he had not defrauded them. The real question was whether this £3,000 policy was really Helen's or Wainewright's. The next point: was there misrepresentation? If there had been, then Wainewright could not win.

The judge did not go on for too long for it was by nearly now nine o'clock at night; the trial had dragged on all day. The jury were out for close to nearly two hours. At 10.30pm one of the ushers came into the court and told the judge that they were divided - six - to six and there was no prospect of their coming to a decision. Solicitors for both sides consulted and agreed to end the hearing. It had lasted fourteen hours.

Wainewright heard the news in France: had he won the case, Madalina would have benefitted and the other insurance companies would have to follow the precedent and shell out, which meant that he could gain too, as the policies in the Hope and Palladium which had been assigned to him would net him £8,000, though being a hunted felon would make it difficult if not impossible to claim what was due to him.

In the meantime, Madalina would have to wait until the case was resolved at another trial.

The mounting expense of all this was exercising the Imperial and in chambers, Sir Frederick Pollock submitted to three judges an affidavit seeking security for costs and asking for the new proceedings to be stayed. The affidavit declared that Wainewright was abroad and unlikely to return because charges of forgery would be brought against him. But the Attorney-general admitted that this was already known before the hearing and on a technicality, lost his application.

There would have to be another expensive trial.

## CHAPTER 14

## "THE INMATE OF AN EARLY TOMB"

The second hearing took place five months later on December 3, 1835. Lord Abinger again presided. This time the court was to hear from the other insurance companies as well as the Imperial.

Much of the evidence was repetition of what he had heard in June. But the defence had altered ground. The main attack was now to be on misrepresentation not murder by poison. But Wainewright's counsel, Mr Erle, did not know this as he plunged in with his opening speech: "I am aware of the nature of the defence; a more foul and unjustifiable one has never been made in a court of law". The Attorney-general answered him later.

Mr Erle now tried to show that Helen was not as destitute as his opponent had made out. She was the daughter of a deceased meritorious officer in the Army. Her mother had owned property. And the reason she had contracted a two-year policy was because a suit in Chancery was expected to be decided in her favour.

This, of course, was what Helen had told the Alliance - who had refused to insure her. Erle was on very thin ice, an explanation patently contrived at the time of the insurances was being repeated. But the other side did not raise any questions: which suit, in what court and at whose bidding?

Erle's best witnesses were Dr Locock and Hanks the apothecary who again attributed the death to oysters and wet feet. There was no suspicion of foul play, testified Hanks.

The defence opened with a new Attorney-general, Sir John Campbell who had replaced Sir Frederick Pollock, conceding the poisoning issue that had been raised by his predecessor: "I beg to relieve the jury from the apprehension excited in their minds that it was my intention to impute to the plaintiff, or parties connected with him, the murder of Miss Abercromby.

Note the "or parties connected with him". He could only have been referring to Eliza, who had been accused in the previous hearing of administering the 'fatal cup'. He was now withdrawing the suggestion because it had upset the judge in the previous hearing who had ruled that even if it had been murder, it was irrelevant to the claim against the Imperial.

He broadened the case out to include all the policies, not just the Imperial and went on: " I contend that my clients are entitled to a verdict on two grounds: firstly that Miss Abercromby and Mrs Wainewright made false statements to the insurance offices and secondly that Miss Abercromby had no interest in the policy which was effected for Wainewright's benefit." She did not even have the money to pay the premiums on the many policies which had been raised.

Sir John got into his stride: "Though in blooming health when those policies were effected, yet not more than a month elapsed before she was the inmate of an early tomb".

The whole transaction, he said, was of a most suspicious nature; "Mr Wainewright has left this country and there is good reason to believe that he will never return again."

To prove Wainewright's charge of fraudulent representation and suppression of facts, Sir John produced a series of witnesses, the actuaries and secretaries of the various companies that Helen had visited, the lawyers who had drawn up the wills and forms transferring the policies.

They told their stories of how they were - or were not - taken in; of the differing tales Helen and Eliza had told at the various offices. Henry Cornwall, Sharpus' lawyer, told of the two wills.

Finally it was the turn of the sadder but wiser tradesmen of Turnham Green. The butcher, the baker, the grocer and the coal merchant testified that Wainewright was indebted to them. The butcher claimed to be owed £200 for meat - a fantastic sum, Wainewright had not even properly paid his own servants. Sarah Handcocks, Dr Griffiths' old servant, now in Madalina's household, told how she had worked for Wainewright and known him since he was a child and said she was never paid regularly and was still owed money five years after his disappearance to France.

There was not much left for Erlc to say, only to repeat lamely that the insurances were perfectly legal; Helen had wanted to provide for her sister if she became destitute. The aspersions cast on Wainewright were totally unfounded. No mention here of the fatal dose administered by Eliza.

Lord Abinger summed up: there were two points for the jury to consider - was there misrepresentation at the Imperial office and was the insurance really for Wainewright's benefit, rather than Helen's, thus contravening the law? The case, he said, was pregnant with suspicion.

He could not presume that Helen had been done away with and it was not necessary to consider whether murder had been committed, because that would not prevent Wainewright from getting the money, providing that the insurance had been effected *bona fide* on her behalf.

But there was the extraordinary fact that the insurance was only for two years and not a tittle of proof had been given to substantiate the reasons for this she had given to the various offices.

He went on: "By the assignments and wills made by Miss Abercromby, Mr Wainewright was placed in a situation in which the law will not allow any person to stand - namely that of having an interest in procuring the death of a fellow creature."

The jury had no doubts this time; they returned a verdict immediately for the Imperial; there had been misrepresentations, they declared, and Helen had no real interest in the insurance.

Wainewright and Eliza's stratagems of five years previously had come to nothing - the deceit, the misrepresentations and the murder were all in vain; neither they nor the innocent Madalina would benefit by a penny.

She had lost a mother and a sister and tragedy was to continue to dog her life. Her marriage to Benjamin Wheatley, who had sold off the contents of Linden House and become both a relative and creditor of Wainewright, was short-lived.

The *Times* of September 28th 1837 reported:

THE FATAL CUP

*We regret to hear that Mr Wheatley the well-known auctioneer in Piccadilly has met his death by falling from his gig on his head. Death almost immediately followed He has left a large family.*

A week later the *Times* had more information on the tragedy from the *Lincoln Gazette*. Wheatley, a Lincolnshire man, and Madalina had been to visit his relatives at the Reindeer Inn in Louth. Madalina had wanted to see the countryside so he had hired a four-wheeled phaeton and a boy to drive it.

*Mr Wheatley had cause to complain of the boy's furious driving, but he, regardless of all remonstrances, continued to flog the horse.*

Trying to negotiate a corner the carriage overturned, crushing Wheatley beneath it. He died the next day in the local pub. The boy escaped with slight injuries; Madalina was "recovering from the ordeal though suffering great affliction at her sudden and awful bereavement".

Wheatley had children by his previous marriage, another two by Madalina, and then seven months after his death she gave birth to another boy, who was named Henry Benjamin after his father.

Tragedy continued. The children were soon to become orphans as Madalina died of scarlet fever and was buried in June 1839 at St Luke's, Chelsea. She was barely 30 years old.

# CHAPTER 15

# AN EXTRAORDINARY OFFER OF BETRAYAL

After the trial, there was silence for a few months. In France, Wainewright sponged on his friends and painted; in London, the Bank of England smarted at their failure. Then, in April 1836, an extraordinary letter arrived in London from Dunkirk, addressed to "Freshfield Esq. M.P., Solicitor to the Bank of England." It was an offer to betray Wainewright to the authorities - for money. It has lain undiscovered in the archives of the Bank for more than 150 years and has never been published before.

Posted Dunkerque 15 April 1836

To: Freshfield Esq. M.P.

Solicitors to the Bank
of England, London

*Sir,*
*I understand you want Thomas Wainewright. You may and shall have in 10 days if you think he is worth the money. Behold my terms. For my part £60 will do, but he will cost more tho' none of it will go into my pocket or thro' my hands, worse luck. You have got a humbugging set of chattering fools, (Forrester's no good!), who are no match for him and if you don't look*

*sharp you'll lose him altogether. I know what track he is on and my scheme is sure, sure! I am neither a nose nor a blood hunter, and why I seek to trap him is nothing to anyone, but so much I'll say, that it is not for lucre (tho' I must have some for needful expenses). While he is loose there's no rest or safety for me.*

*Now to business. First a Twenty pound note (earnest money) directed M. Auguste, Poste Restante, Dunkerque. Next send off instantly a clever gentlemanly man to await my communication at the Hotel de Flandres here. I shall inquire for Mr Stone. If he meets W there before he sees or hears from "Auguste" let him commence intimacy over some Bordeaux and state that he comes from some part of W's family, (Wainewright won't ask questions), to assist him in his difficulties with people in Paris.*

*He must affect sympathy with W and hint something about his dark-eyed lady-bird, and ask knowingly after Amalie v. Holst and Graciosa Mechlin. Then if questioned, look mysterious and change the subject and drop something on Prague and Mdlle Saintine, Baron d'Ordre, hope matters are looking better, propose a health to the Exile of Holyrood, and the captive at Blage. This will tickle W like a trout! His full instructions shall be on his dressing table next morning.*

*Of course, you are the judge whether it is worthwhile to risk £20. Do as you like. There is my offer and I am a very different sort of person from your agents with their pettifogging, shallow cunning and damned vulgar faces which carry "trap" stamped on every degraded feature.*

*Damn it, it's almost a pity. He is a noble, charitable, generous and talented creature and one I would have backed against the bloodhounds to the last fragment of my knife. But enough! No hanging an arse now! He is yours if you pay for him. You can't take him by force alive and yr (sic) clumsy owls are not the men to come over so wide-awake a cove as Wainewright.*

*If I get no satisfactory answer by Monday I shall conclude it's not go and shall leave Dunkerque after making my peace with him. (I know all your Calais and old Boulogne manoeuvres).*

*One hint more I give you. He wants to be in England for three or four days and they ask him too much for smuggling him in disguise there and back. His mistress is the thing. "Now do you catch the focus?" Make him a golden bridge. There is his weak point. Women! He's outrageously in love and would risk his life fifty times for an interview.*

*This thing must be kept, as may be seen, quite secret and no police blackguards. Don't bring over his servants and bitch the business this time. He knew all along what you were after, but determined to fight it out at Boulogne. Well! you were floored (he saw you there; besides there were lots to tell him. Those pretending to assist have split to him). Enfin, if you don't like very good! I'll not alter my demand or my plan, your man must be under my counsel or it's*

*odds I am not as good at a plot as any blackcoat of you all.*
*Adieu*
Monsieur A
*No friend of yours but an enemy of his. My terms are £20 down, enlistment money, £20 more when going into the boat with your agent and £20 when safe at London.*

*You see that if you risk £20 (only the price of a lottery ticket or a ticket for a weekend Pol) I, your amiable servant, also risk my last payment I could help you to some other that your devils have missed.*

Who was Monsieur Auguste who penned this? An Englishman, obviously, with such a robust style and command of idiom, and obviously very well-read. The reference to a golden bridge comes from the aphorism of the 5th century BC Chinese military strategist Sun Tzu: 'build your opponent a golden bridge to retreat across.' Perhaps he was another of the English renegades living across the Channel, displaying, as he does, a violent contempt for Wainewright's pursuers. A bounty hunter? A friend of Wainewright's yet ready to betray him? "A noble talented and generous creature," he calls him, yet "while he's loose there's no rest or safety for me."

It is curious that Monsieur Auguste addressed the envelope so precisely. He knew that Freshfield acted for the Bank of England, and also that he was an M.P. (He had been elected for the rotten borough of Penryn in Cornwall in 1830). He also knew that Forrester the London City policemen was on Wainewright's tail, and more intriguing is the reference: "Don't bring over his servants and bitch the business this time" which suggests that Sarah Handcocks and Harriet Grattan had been taken to France by Wainewright's pursuers in order to identify him.

Despite the protestations of danger, Auguste obviously needed the money more than his safety. The number of times he mentions his terms are evidence enough of that. The £60 would be many thousands in today's terms. His offer to lead the authorities to other miscreants showed he was in the business of being an informer.

But Auguste could have been Wainewright himself, indulging in an elaborate sting to obtain funds. Perhaps after the first £20 was left at the Dunkirk post office, nothing more would be heard of Auguste and no-one would turn up at the rendezvous at the Hotel de Flandres where they might be arrested.

Some names in the letter are untraceable, but Baron d'Ordre, was as we know, Inspector of Water and Forests in the Pas de Calais and a noted *litterateur*. Just the sort of company Wainewright would have sought and indeed he mentions the baron in one of his petitions.

Amalie v. Holst was Amelia Thomasina Symmes Villard, the favourite model of Wainewright's friend, the painter Theodor Von Holst [1] who was

---

[1] They were not married at the time; she would have been only 16. The Ashmolean Museum in Oxford has in its print room three sketches by Von Holst, one of which has on the back three drawings of him done by Amelia.

later to shelter Wainewright from the law. The Exile of Holyrood may refer to Holyrood Abbey in Edinburgh. It offered the right of sanctuary to those who could not pay their debts, an idea which would appeal to Wainewright.[2]

The records of the Bank of England do not disclose whether they took up Monsieur Auguste's offer. Wainewright did not return to London for another year. But he may well have returned for the same reason, the pursuance of a woman.

"There is his weak point, 'Women!' Barry Cornwall had no doubts about the matter: "(he) became personally intimate with a married female at Calais, whom fear of detection or some other strong motive induced him to poison. Not only was this female fond of him, but her sister also became attached to him and subsequently followed him to England when he returned there." More sisters and another unsubstantiated allegation of poisoning.

W.C. Hazlitt had heard a similar story about the shadowy woman: "I have heard it whispered that a lady was in the question – not Mrs Wainewright, for the husband and wife separated in 1831, to meet no more."

Oscar Wilde saw drama in the situation: "Some strange, mad fascination brought him back. He followed a woman whom he loved... it was said the woman was very beautiful. Besides, she did not love him."

---

[2.] The exile himself was probably the Comte d'Artois, the former Bourbon king Charles X, who fled to Britain after the July revolution of 1830 and lived either in the Abbey or Holyroodhouse which adjoins it.

Perhaps he crossed M. Auguste's 'golden bridge' in vain. Whether Wainewright was lured back or not, he returned in April 1837 and it is significant that a woman features in the account of his arrest given in court.

The least reliable accounts of his capture, given by Wilde and others, has Wainewright in a hotel in Covent Garden. He pushes back the blind for a moment and who is outside the window but the policeman Forrester who cries: "There's Wainewright, the bank forger." Forrester is outside, it's explained, because Bow Street police station, where the Runners were based, was in Covent Garden, opposite the Royal Opera House.

But Forrester was a City policeman and his own account of the arrest puts it near Howland Street, a mile or so from Covent Garden, in a louche area north of Soho and east of Marylebone now known as Fitzrovia, which became notorious later in the century for its brothels and is now known largely for housing the Post Office Tower.

Howland Street was not Forrester's beat; the City Day Police operated, as the City force do now, in their own circumscribed area in the City; this was Metropolitan police territory, so it seems that Forrester had prior knowledge of Wainewright's whereabouts and had the permission to arrest him there.

The painter Fuseli, idolised by Wainewright, lived nearby and so did Fuseli's pupil Von Holst, one of great unsung painters of the Romantic movement. He was admired by his fellow painters but the supernatural and erotic content of his art was disapproved of the bourgeois London public of the 1830s, but he possessed precisely the qualities which would appeal to Wainewright, particularly as almost half his works were based on the German Romantics, who were adored by Wainewright.

.Colnaghi the print-seller, who had had many dealings with Wainewright and his circle, was to write later to Bulwer Lytton the novelist:" Holst (sic) and he (Wainewright) were on the most intimate terms and during the period of his last stay in London, when the police were on his track, he remained hid in Holst's house in Howland Street.".

In fact Von Holst lived just around the corner in Nassau Street, alongside the Middlesex Hospital. It is this covering address which appears on the petitions for mercy to the authorities, which Von Holst put forward on Wainewright's behalf even after transportation.

It was a long time since M Auguste's offer, but the circumstances of the arrest certainly imply that Wainewright was betrayed and that Forrester knew where to find him.

On Saturday, June the 10th, the morning after his arrest, he appeared at Mansion House court in the City. Four morning papers carried the story on Monday; only one of them spelled his name correctly.

**POLICE**

Mansion House. On Saturday a man of respectable appearance, named Thomas Griffiths Wainewright, was brought up, charged with having used a power of attorney for the sale and transfer of £2,250 in the stock of the New Four per Cent Annuities, standing in the names of Robert Wainwrights (sic), of Gray's Inn,

Edward Smith Foss, of Essex Street, Strand, and Edward Foss, of Bernard Street, Russell Square, with intent to defraud the Governor and Company of the Bank of England.

John and Daniel Forrester, the officers, have had a warrant against the prisoner since 1835, and having gone over to Boulogne after him at that time, but without being able to accomplish anything except the object of seeing him, were rather particular in their enquiries as to the probable time of his return to this country.

On Friday evening Daniel Forrester, having observed a female whom he knew to be a friend of the prisoner in the neighbourhood of Howland Street, cautiously looked about, followed her, and soon saw her joined by a person whom, notwithstanding the addition of a large tuft of mustachios and beard, he know to be the prisoner; he ran up, and tapping him smartly on the arm, said, 'Ah, Mr Wainewright, how do you do? Who would have thought of seeing you here?"

The prisoner started upon being thus addressed, and was what is called completely flummoxed, did not deny that he was the man, and was locked up in the Compter. He had about him a small dirk in a sheath, and appeared to be without money or friends.

Sir Peter Laurie (who sat for the Lord Mayor) asked the prisoner what he was:

*Prisoner – I am nothing. I have been an independent gentleman, and had considerable property, and I was originally an officer in the 16th Foot.*

*Sir Peter Laurie – Have you been here long? I see you are described in the warrant as an artist.*

*Prisoner – I am no artist. I belong to no trade or profession, and have been in France these six or seven years. I arrived here about six weeks ago.*

Mr Freshfield, solicitor to the Bank of England, called witnesses to prove the case so far as to justify the Alderman in remanding the prisoner.

Mr Jonas Rogers Woodford, a clerk in the Bank of England, produced the bank ledger, in which was kept the account of Robert Wainright (sic), Edward Smith Foss, and Edward Foss, from which it appeared that £5,000 in Navy 5% had been converted into the new 4% annuities on the 5th of July, 1822. The total amount was £5,250; that on the 15th of July 1822, (it was May 12, 1823 in some accounts) £2,250 of that sum had been transferred, and on the 17th of May 1824 the remaining sum of £3,000 was paid out. The transfer papers, were witnessed by a Mr Catteron, a clerk in the Bank, since deceased, and signed T.G. Wainewright.

Mr Edward Foss stated that he was one of the trustees of the stock described. His father, who was now dead, had been another, and Mr Robert Wainewright was a third trustee. The signatures of witness and his father were forged.

*Sir P Laurie – Prisoner, do you wish to ask any questions?*

*Prisoner – None at all at present. I am not yet steady in my head; I was arrested but yesterday, and have not had time to communicate with my friends.*

*Sir P Laurie – The charge is a serious one; do you wish for time?*

*Prisoner - I shall have to send to France for documents and wish to be remanded.*

*Sir P Laurie – You shall be remanded till the latter end of the next week.*

*Sir P Laurie said he thought the Bank might prevent losses such as they had sustained in the present instance by writing to the joint trustees in all cases of transfer.*

Here he was - the perfumed, lisping dandy - in a state of degradation, penniless, armed with a small dagger, and apparently in a condition of great despondency – even denying that he was an artist. "I am nothing... I belong to no trade or profession."

He was sent back to the Compter, the small City gaol across the Thames in Southwark.

While he was there, King William IV, 'Silly Billy', died at Windsor on June 20 and Queen Victoria acceded to the throne, news which filled the papers for days which is why there is nothing can be found about his committal to the Old Bailey at the Mansion House court on June 23, proceedings which would have disclosed much more about his doings.

From the Compter he was moved to the infamous prison at Newgate. There, in the summer of 1837, he waited for his trial.

## CHAPTER 16

## THE 'WRETCHED WAINEWRIGHT' IN NEWGATE

The "Great Inimitable Mr Dickens" was 25 and had already began his leap to fame. *Sketches by Boz* had been well received; *Pickwick Papers*, after a disappointing response to the first of the shilling instalments, was making a fortune for its publishers, Chapman and Hall. *Oliver Twist* was underway in *Bentley's Miscellany* which Dickens was also editing at £40 a month.

Already beginning to show signs of strain, he was also planning *Gabriel Vardon, The Locksmith of London*, which, in spite of his prodigious output, did not appear for another four years – and then under a different title, *Barnaby Rudge*.

The central feature was to be Newgate – then, as for years to come, one of the worst prisons in Britain. "We can never pass the building without something like a shudder", Dickens had written in the *Sketches*.

Prisons played a large part in his life, he was almost obsessed by them. Visiting his importunate father in the Marshalsea debtors' prison in Southwark not many years before had left an indelible impression upon him.

He had visited Newgate and written about it in *Great Expectations*. Now, collecting material for *Gabriel Vardon*, he was going there again – his visit arranged by the same Sir Peter Laurie who had remanded Wainewright at Mansion House.[1]

By the mid-thirties Newgate was mainly a remand prison. A Government inquiry of the time reported that the prisoners slept three or four to a cell on rope mats on the floor, huddled together for warmth and covered with dirty stable rugs. Their diet was of the cheapest and poorest.

However, they had it easy, according to a Lords' select committee report on prisons in 1835. "We noticed scarcely anything in the apartments that indicated the discomfort and privations of a place of penal confinement." Clean linen, beer and newspapers were brought in and prostitutes visited. Bibles and prayer books were available "but they showed little sign of having been used".

Prisoners who were rich could stay in the governor's lodgings at the cost of a guinea a day (about £50 at present values) and have their food brought in.

However in the year Wainewright was remanded there, conditions improved markedly. A report of the improvements dated September 1837 said there was now a bed for every prisoner, there was a bath (sic) on the male and female side of the prison and there were now arrangements for fumigating prisoners' clothes.

On that summer's day – June 27, 1837 – Dickens had already been to Coldbath Fields Prison in Clerkenwell – where whipping was common and

---

[1.] Dickens repaid him ill, lampooning him in *The Chimes* as Alderman Cute. His insensitivity also made him the favourite butt of *Punch* throughout the 1840s.

women could be seen in the treadmill. With him were his new friend John Forster. the critic who became his biographer; William Macready, the actor-manager, both well known to Wainewright as they had dined at his table, and Hablot Knight Browne, the "Phiz" who illustrated *Pickwick.*

In tall beaver hats and frock coats, the four stooped to enter the small lodge door of Newgate, then, as the bolts were shot behind them, they went through the massive inner doors into the gloom and stench of the stone corridors.

Suddenly there was a shout. Forster recalled it later: "We were startled by a sudden cry of 'My God, there's Wainewright'. They saw a "shabby genteel creature with sandy, disordered hair and dirty moustache, who had turned quickly round with a defiant stare at our entrance, looking at once both mean and fierce". Forster was writing this many years later, his description coloured by the moralising tone which former friends of Wainewright adopted after his conviction and transportation.

Macready had been horrified to recognise a man familiarly known to him in former years and whose hospitality he had enjoyed. In his *Reminiscences* he gave more details of the incident: "I looked through an eyelet hole in one of cells where there were four prisoners, and to my surprise, and, I may say, horror, among them distinguished the features of the wretched Wainewright."

Macready was quick to add that he had had only a brief friendship with Wainewright and that 20 years before. The party passed on, but the incident had made a deep impression on Dickens, and more than 20 years later it made him a thousand pounds, a huge advance, which he got for a short story, *Hunted Down*, a tale of insurance, poisoning and death, said to have been inspired by Wainewright's crimes.

Oscar Wilde wrote: "His cell was for some time a kind of fashionable lounge. Many men of letters went to visit their old literary comrade." To one of his guests, Wainewright was supposed to have said: "They pay me respect here, I assure you. They think I am here for ten-thousand pounds."

To another, he made his most famous, and probably apocryphal remark. Asked how he could have killed such an innocent as Helen Abercromby, he replied: "Upon my soul I don't know – unless it was that her ankles were too thick." In some versions of the story it is her legs that are too thick. It is a quotation probably invented by John Camden Hotten, who was the publisher in 1860 of Dickens' *Hunted Down which* was based on the Wainewright case. Hotten wrote a foreword to it and was not backward when it came to publicity for his publications.

The remark is more redolent of Oscar Wilde's cynicism or even that of another famous dandy Beau Brummel, who, when asked when asked why he had jilted a beauty replied: "What else could I do? I found she actually ate cabbage."

One of his visitors, named as "a man from Lombard Street", is said to have asked Wainewright if he now realised if, purely as a speculation, crime did not pay. To this, he is said to have replied:

*Sir, you City men enter on your speculations and take the chances of them. Some of your speculations succeed, some fail. Mine happen to have failed, yours happen to have succeeded; that is the difference, Sir, between my visitor and me. But I'll tell you one thing in which I have succeeded to the last. I have been determined through life to hold the position of a gentleman. I have always done so, I do so still. It is the custom of this place that each of the inmates of a cell shall take his morning's turn of sweeping out. I occupy a cell with a bricklayer and a sweep. But, by God, they never offer me the broom!*

Unless whoever heard this took a shorthand note, its accuracy is doubtful, as is its provenance. But it still conveys the flavour of the man.

A more important visitor was the indefatigable Thompson. The insurance companies had not finished with Wainewright. In December 1836, while he was still in France, Madalina's lawyers had decided to sue the Eagle and Pelican companies for the sums due to her under the policies negotiated by her brother-in-law. The directors of both companies –seeing a clear precedent in Lord Abinger's judgement for the Imperial a year before – decided at once to resist the claim.

In the early months of 1837, the Eagle's solicitors, Le Blanc, Oliver and Cook were drawing up the case. Then – a stroke of luck – Wainewright was arrested. The Eagle knew that if they could get Wainewright to swear that the policy had been fraudulently negotiated, Madalina would have to abandon the case.

Thompson went to Wainewright's cell; what took place there we cannot tell. Wainewright seems not to have specifically admitted his guilt in writing, though he does seem to have agreed that there was fraud involved. He gave permission for his papers to be collected from France by the Eagle's solicitors. The minutes of the Eagle take up the story:

*1837 July 19: That Messrs. Le Blanc, Oliver and Cook be authorised to despatch a person to Boulogne, St. Omer, Paris and such other places as may be requisite, to inspect or release T.G. Wainewright's papers, under the written authority to that effect given to Mr Thompson.*

*"The declaration of T.G. Wainewright respecting the policy on Miss Abercromby was read."*

## CHAPTER 17

## IN THE DOCK

On Wednesday July 5, 1837, Mr Sergeant Arabin took his seat in the Old Court at the Old Bailey at nine in the morning. The first prisoner put up by the gaoler was Thomas Griffiths Wainewright, "a man of very gentlemanly appearance" recorded the *Chronicle*. He pleaded not guilty to four charges. Two of them were capital, carrying the death penalty, alleging forgery of the powers of attorney to obtain a total of £5,250; two were non-capital, charging that he "feloniously, knowingly and fraudulently" got hold of the money through the forgery. This distinction was to be important, if not vital.

At this stage, the course of events becomes obscure. Wainewright, having declared his innocence, was suddenly put down again, and in a cell, according to him, he was "trepanned (thro' the just, but deluded Governor of Newgate) into withdrawing his plea, by a promise, in such case, of a punishment merely nominal."

The approach, purported to come, said Wainewright, from the Bank of England, but in fact was from the insurance companies "interested to a heavy amount (£16,000) in compassing his legal non-existence".

At ten o'clock he appeared in court again, this time before Mr Justice Vaughan, and changed his plea to guilty on all counts. The prosecution offered no evidence on the two capital charges and proceeded only with the lesser. What had happened in that hour beneath the court? Why did the Governor of Newgate, a Mr Cope, intervene?

There were two major factors which were influencing the outcome of the case – the embarrassing position of the Bank, who had not detected the fraud for years, and the insurance companies' unfinished business against Wainewright, still pursuing them nominally as the legal executor of Helen's estate on behalf of Madalina.

The withdrawal of two charges and a guilty plea to the others meant that no evidence had to be given and an instant trial suited the Bank. It was spared the embarrassment of having the facts emerge about how it had been duped so easily and for so long, not to mention a recital of the farcical attempts to bring Wainewright back to England.

There was also some sensitivity about hanging a man for an offence committed 13 years earlier, given that at the time of his appearance, a Bill to end capital punishment for further categories of offences was being piloted through the Commons by the Home Secretary Lord John Russell. It included the abolition of the death penalty for the very capital offences of which he had twice been charged - forging a power of attorney.

The Bank's attitude had changed greatly since the early years of the century, when it prosecuted relentlessly on forgery charges. Between 1807 and 1818, there had been a total 207 executions for forgery - more than for murder, burglary or robbery from the person. Crimes against property in Georgian England were punished savagely.[1]

In *The Chronicles of Newgate*, Arthur Griffiths wrote:

*It may be remarked that the Bank of England was by far the bitter and most implacable as regards prosecution for forgery. Of the above-mentioned 207 executions for this crime, no less than 72 were the victims of proceedings instituted by the Bank.*

But their attitude had softened, according to a history of the Bank.[2] They sometimes helped financially the families of men who had been executed for fraud and the prosecution committee had several times asked the Home Secretary if those to be transported could take their families with them.

At the brief hearing, the Bank's recently-appointed standing counsel, Mr Maule, (who appears later in the Wainewright story), said they no desire whatever to press the capital charges. There was no wish to forfeit the life of the prisoner, so no evidence would be offered.

---

[1] On the same page of the *Newgate Calendar* as Wainewright's presence is recorded, is that of Henry Goody, transported for seven years for "stealing a handkerchief from a person unknown". He was 15 years old.

[2] Acres. *The Bank of England from Within*

From the Bench, Mr Justice Vaughan joined in: he was able to bear testimony to the great humanity of the Bank and to the anxiety with which they always endeavoured to avoid the shedding of blood. He had himself been counsel for the Bank for many years and knew how merciful they were.

After this display of mutual wonder at the Bank's altruism, Wainewright was formally found guilty and sent back to his cell to await sentence.

The Eagle's actuary, Henry P. Smith, writing to Bulwer Lytton, nine years later, declared: "He was allowed by the Bank to plead guilty to the second plea....which saved his life."

But what really persuaded Wainewright to plead guilty was the offer of intercession by the insurance companies, led by Smith of the Eagle. It became widely known and was mentioned by Walter Thornbury in his lurid *Old Stories Re-Told*, published in 1870, and again by a contributor to *Leisure Hour* writing 20 years later who said: "To defeat her (Madalina's) claim, Wainewright entered into communication with the insurance companies who promised that they would represent his case to the Secretary of State. That representation, however, instead of mitigating Wainewright's punishment, increased it."

He had to wait two more days to be told his fate. On Friday the 7th, at the end of the sessions, the Recorder brought in front of him at four in the afternoon all those on whom sentence had been postponed.

At the first hearing, Wainewright had not spoken other than to plead to the charges. He had not had any opportunity to say anything in mitigation of his offences which might make his sentence lighter – after all he had been promised a nominal punishment.

He tried now to speak, but the Recorder cut him off - he said he had no power to mitigate or alter the sentence which was to be passed, only the Home Secretary could do that. What he had not been told in that hour below the court was that the offences to which he was persuaded to plead guilty carried a mandatory sentence – there was no possibility of it being a light punishment.

For Wainewright and eleven others the sentence was 'transportation beyond the seas for the extent of their lives and the Recorder, seeing them as desperate men with nothing left to lose, gave them a dire warning about their behaviour in the colonies.

The *Morning Post*, alone of the London newspapers, noted:

*(he) observed upon their conduct in committing crimes which severed them from home and kindred. He impressed upon them the necessity of good conduct hereafter, for most assuredly if they exhibited insubordination to lawful authority their punishment would be increased in a very fearful manner.*

The 12 must have wondered what, short of execution, could be more fearful than the punishment that lay ahead.

The sentence was a great shock, promises had not been kept. Wainewright was outraged at what he saw as a betrayal. He was to describe what had happened as "ruthless perfidy", and for the rest of his life displayed no gratitude for having being spared a hanging. He was extremely lucky that the frauds had not been detected at the time they took place in the early 1820s, for he assuredly would have been executed.[3]

There is a curiosity in the sentence book; Wainewright's name is bracketed with one Eugene Aram, 18, transported for life, who was to accompany him on his trip to the other side of the world. "Eugene" - almost certainly adopting a false name - had gone to see a Dr Conquest in Finsbury Square, but instead of waiting for the consultation had made off with a cloak and small desk. His unusual name was also the title of an 1832 book by Bulwer Lytton based on the notorious philosopher-murderer Eugene Aram, who was hanged in 1759 for killing a shoemaker. Lytton, of course, was to base another of his books, *Lucretia or Children of the Night*, on Wainewright.

The Bank may well have been satisfied by the sentence; the insurance companies were not. Although they had won on the second trial in the Imperial case, two other suits against the Pelican and the Eagle were still pending. Wainewright's conviction made no difference and he was about to be sent to the other side of the world. Henry Smith of the Eagle still had work to do and time was running out.

---

[3.] There were 364 people hanged in England between 1821 and 1825; three-quarters were convicted of property crimes while only a fifth of those convicted of murder met the same fate, according to Richard Evans' *The Pursuit of Power, Europe 1815-1914*.

On July 11, 1837, the Home Office sent an authorisation to Newgate to remove Wainewright to the prison hulk *York* lying at Gosport, in Portsmouth harbour, there to await his transportation.

# CHAPTER 18

# AN OFFER TO TELL ALL

Now came two desperate moves by Wainewright to save himself from his fate. Time was fast running out and in the days before he was put aboard the convict ship to Van Diemen's land he made two dramatic moves - firstly an appeal for mercy to the Home Secretary and secondly an extraordinary offer to tell all about the events leading to Helen's death, contained in a document in the National Archives that has never been published before.

While Henry Smith continued his machinations to end the civil court proceedings against the Eagle insurance company by trying to detect foul play in Helen's death, Wainewright appealed against his forgery conviction to the Home Secretary, Lord John Russell, from what he called "his most unhappy and degraded situation". The grounds for appeal were simple; although he could not excuse his crimes, they were mere technicalities, as the money was really his all the time.

His petition (Appendix 1), is also preserved in the National Archives and begins by complaining in perfect cursive script, probably the work of a copying clerk, about the conduct of the case:

> ...although your petitioner pleaded guilty, he was still desirous that the whole Circumstances of the Transactions should be known to the Court in hopes that the Judgment to be passed

*upon him might possibly be affected thereby and when called up to receive sentence Your Petitioner applied to the presiding Judge, the Recorder of the City of London, who referred the Petitioner to your Lordship saying he had no power to alter or mitigate the sentence to be passed....*

He continued by saying that at an early age (he was then, in fact, 23) he had formed a very "injudicious marriage without the knowledge of any of his relations" which soon led him into "difficulties and Embarrassments", but to guard against "further involving himself", as he put it, he was induced to settle £5,000 (*it was eventually £5,250*) on his wife for the benefit of any children that they might have.... but if there was a "failure of issue" it would be in trust for him. (The embarrassment mentioned here is not emotional discomfiture but lack of money).

In the meantime, the dividends on this capital sum were paid to him through the trustees, but as he phrased it "to save trouble" he had been given the power of attorney to receive them directly. It was not given to him, of course, he forged the documents.

He then laid out in the third person, as the petitioner, the nub of his case:

*In the Year 1823, his Wife then having no Children altho' several years Married* (it was six) *and your Petitioner considering that he would eventually by the Terms of this settlement become entitled to the Money, and being embarrassed Committed the Crime.*

> ....although Your Petitioner seeks not to excuse the Crime, he yet ventures to suggest as a palliation that the Money obtained was originally his own and placed in the hands of Trustees for a specific object which had then not occurred nor was there any probability of such occurrence.

He called upon the Home Secretary's humane consideration to interfere to soften the rigour of his sentence consistent with humanity and justice.

He was being economical with the truth. There was, for instance, the crucial omission in this self-serving saga of son Griffiths, now 11 years old and deprived of his inheritance by his father's forgeries.

While his petition would its way through the bureaucratic toils of the Home Office, Smith was pursuing his own ends. He had no doubt that if the cases went against the Eagle and the Pelican, which would have to pay out a total of £8,000, (£820,000) the Palladium and the Hope would have to pay out the same and those proceeds had been legally assigned to Wainewright in December 1830, before Helen's death.

Smith had amassed a great deal on information about Wainewright's exile through Thompson's visits to France, including an alleged verbal confession to Helen's murder. But he now hoped to get conclusive proof of the killing from the material Wainewright had left behind in France.

Thompson and Smith had both visited him there and had been given permission by Wainewright to have his papers confiscated. The Eagle's solicitors sent someone to Boulogne, Paris, St Omer and other places to retrieve them. By the end of July they had collected the majority, but there was no incriminating evidence, so Smith himself was then sent back to Paris and Boulogne to retrieve what remained.

It was not straightforward, as whoever had the papers would not release them until Wainewright's lodging debts were paid. The British consul in Boulogne was instructed to pay 280 francs to release them and send them to the Eagle's offices.

The total haul filled several trunks with books, drawings and papers, but there was still nothing of substance for Smith, who, ever indefatigable in his company's service, visited Wainewright in his cell and struck a bargain, which could – on certain terms – end the insurance cases and free the Eagle, and by precedent, the other companies, from having to pay out enormous sums.

There was now even less time left as Wainewright was about to begin his journey to the south coast to the convict ship which was to waiting to take him to the other end of the world and into exile for life.

On Monday, July 17th, 1837, Smith and the Eagle's solicitor, Cook went to the Home Office with a letter Smith had written, which is still preserved in Home Office files in the National Archive, laying out the bargain with Wainewright.

It contains the extraordinary offer by Wainewright to tell all - but only in return for a free pardon, something which could be granted only by the recommendation of the Home Secretary to the sovereign, Queen Victoria, who had acceded to the throne the previous month.

Firstly, Smith laid out the story of the forgeries and the death of Helen, noting with irritation that the judge in the first civil trial had "interfered and prevented the Defendant's counsel from going into the circumstances of the death", for Lord Abinger had firmly ruled out any evidence which suggested poisoning, as being irrelevant to the forgery case he was hearing.

Then Smith went on to say that he had recently seen Wainewright and...

> ....he has offered that if his safety be guaranteed, and a free pardon be granted to him, to enable him to give Evidence, he will make a full disclosure of all the facts connected with the concoction of this Fraud, and the death of Miss Abercromby. Considering the large amount of property which is at stake, and the strange mystery which attaches to this and other cases in which Wainewright appears to have been connected, I have felt it my duty to make his offer known to the Secretary of State.

This was the bargain, the promised intercession which could free Wainewright from his sentence, a guarantee he would not be charged with anything else and the insurance companies would be relieved from their obligations.

Free pardons are now extremely rare and it seems ludicrous that a convict should demand one within days of being sentenced, but it was quite common for such pardons to be granted in the nineteenth century. For example in the five months to July 1837, 40 free pardons had been signed by the Home Secretary, Lord John Russell, a notable reformer. Only two weeks or so before Wainewright's offer, one Philip Castree, being held in the *Ganymede* hulk at Woolwich and about to be transported for a felony, had been freed unconditionally.

It is clear that such accommodations were as a result of co-operation with the authorities, so Wainewright's hopes were not necessarily vain. But the hours were passing, and Wainewright's desperation was increasing. Five days later, on Saturday, July 22nd, a letter arrived at the Eagle's solicitors marked 'private' and addressed to one of the clerks.

Wainewright was making the offer again – this time in writing in person. By the time the letter arrived he was already aboard the prison hulk in Gosport awaiting transfer to the convict ship.

The clerk copied out the relevant portion, but not alas the whole letter, and it was sent immediately to the Home Office to the Superintendent of Convicts, John Henry Capper. It is published here for the first time:

> *Am I to hear further from Mr Smith, on the subject of my giving a full account and revelation of the circumstances connected with the sudden or somewhat sudden end of x x.* (sic)
>
> *I am ready. I can point out places where Medicines were procured etc etc. It will you must see complete your affair.*
>
> *However if all what was said meant nothing please to let me know as I must go to work a different way.*
>
> *My evidence will touch two Persons and the Warrants should be got at once to stop further proceedings in Equity.*

*I have been held in awe on account of this business for which I am here. Now all cause of concealment is done away and you may inform the Secretary of State that I am ready to make such depositions as will put Mrs W's affair already very strange in a new light.*

*You must act at once or you will lose one if not both of the people. I have reason to think that they have some suspicion.*

Smith's letter to the Home Office was written, as was the Wainewright extract, by his copy clerk. The underlined cursive letter *W* in the phrase identifying his wife is identical to the same writer's capital *W* in Smith's other correspondence sent to the Home Office by the clerk.

However, more significant is the fact that the letter is a virtual acknowledgement that Helen was poisoned - it admits medicines were bought, but Wainewright himself is not making a confession to murder. He is putting the blame on two others, though there is a sense of his complicity in a crime, as he says all cause of concealment are no longer necessary.

Who are the two people to be to be arrested as they might be preparing to flee? And why now? Presumably because he was now in custody in England rather than in exile in France and was in a position to name names.

*Cui bono?* Who benefited from the crime - and who would need to flee? The Latin phrase crucial to criminal investigations would have suspicion naturally falling on wife Eliza, who administered the fatal dose to her sister and was her husband's co-conspirator in the insurance frauds.

Then there was Helen's sister Madalina, who would gain through Helen's will; there were the servants Sarah Handcocks and Harriet Grattan, who had been unpaid for months. It would hardly be son Griffiths; he was just a young boy. There would have been two others who would have benefitted - Atkinson and his partner Acheson to whom Wainewright had assigned some of the policies. They stood to gain, but they were a respectable firm of solicitors in the City. There were no likely candidates about to do a bunk.

We do not know who Wainewright might have named, perhaps there never were two guilty parties, other than Wainewright and Eliza, and that the offer of confession was just an attempt to buy time.

There is the telling phrase that if this explanation does not fit "I must go to work a different way", which suggests another, different story. It is much like his declaration to his creditors about Helen's two wills - if one failed, the other would do.

But there was to be only a week before the convict ship sailed and this last desperate gambit failed, as did Smith's scheme to save the Eagle's finances. There is no record of what the Home Office decided, not even in its Private and Secret Entry Book for the period which is preserved in the National Archives, but the Home Secretary Lord John Russell did not intervene.

The Register of Criminal Petitions entry, which relates to the petition, not to the subsequent offer of confession, records: Result - Nil. The petition itself has scrawled upon it "Gaol Rept. Connexion respectable" and in a different hand "sailed with Ship *Susan*".

# CHAPTER 19

# THE LAST JOURNEY

Years later in a petition to a Governor of Van Diemen's Land, Wainewright recorded that after conviction he was *"hurried...to the hulks at Portsmouth and thence, in five days, aboard the Susan sentenced to life in a land (to him) a moral sepulchre"*.
There is some exaggeration in this; he was not hurried to Portsmouth, but sent back to Newgate for at least a week after conviction until a party was made up to travel to the hulks. With a heavy guard and escorted by an official from Newgate, the convicts went slowly to Gosport at the mouth of Portsmouth harbour, where the hulks *Leviathan* and *York* were used as a transit camp for the deportation of criminals to the other side of the world and as an overflow system for overcrowded gaols on the mainland.
The hulks at that time have been described as a "hell on earth of violence, disease and squalor". Conditions were far worse than in gaols, which were grim enough. The *York*, to which Wainewright was transferred, had been stationed at Gosport on the western side of the harbour since 1819. She was used for nearly 30 years until she was broken up in 1848 by the forced labour of the prisoners and convicts who lived aboard her.
There was a distinction between the two terms; all gaoled offenders were known as prisoners, but those sentenced to penal servitude – that is

In Portsmouth harbour, convicts are being put aboard the York prison ship. Wainewright would have made this very journey as he was held in the York while waiting transportation to Van Diemen's Land. The York was a decommissioned naval vessel that served as a prison hulk for 30 years and held about 500 convicts. The hulks were notorious for disease and squalor. This etching is by E. W. Cooke.
*National Maritime Museum*

hard labour – or who were to be transported, were called convicts.

Wainewright's arrival was noted in *The Globe* of July 17, 1837:

*This morning 25 convicts were drafted off and conveyed to the York hulk lying at Gosport preparatory to their voyage to New South Wales (sic) to which colony the greater portion of them are banished for life, and of that number is Mr G H Wainwright (sic)......The connexions of this convict are highly respectable, and owing to his contrition and some mitigating circumstances connected with his case, it is believed the sentence will be very considerable mitigated should his future conduct warrant it.*

Convict 2325 Wainewright was fortunate in being only a few days aboard the hulk: most of the 570 prisoners were spending their lives in her. The record of his short time there is both perfunctory and inaccurate.

In the Register of the *York* one of the few facts that was noted correctly was under the heading "Read or Write". In Wainewright's column is scrawled "Superior". His age is given as 40, instead of 42; his occupation as "labourer" and the date of his sentence put back three months to April the 3rd. Perhaps details like this were unimportant in the stinking uproar of the *York*, with a constant flow of men being shipped away, never to be seen again.

It was one more step in the degradation of the dandy. The essayist Charles Lamb's biographer Talfourd quotes a letter written while Wainewright was in the *York*; its recipient is not known.

*They call me a desperado. Me! the companion of poets, philosophers, artists and musicians - a desperado! You will smile at this. No, I think you will feel for the man educated and reared as a gentleman, now the mate of vulgar ruffians and country bumpkins.*

Twenty-four years earlier, the barque *Susan*, a regular on the transportation run, had been built on a crude slipway in Calcutta. A sturdy 573 tons, she lay swinging at anchor at Spithead. The East

Indiamen like the *Susan* made adequate transports. Teak-built, they were roomier than the earlier British-built transports, but they were also dark, evil-smelling and poorly-ventilated.

The Admiralty laid down basic conditions for the transportation of felons and contracted private ship-owners to carry them. But with a burgeoning and profitable private market for transporting voluntary emigrants to America or Australia, the Admiralty's less generous terms meant that they did not get the best ships.

For days supply boats had come tossing out from the quays of Portsmouth with kegs of water, barrels of meat and boxes of biscuits. The first convict ships to New South Wales had stopped to provision at ports like Madeira, Rio and Cape Town, but now most transports made the voyage without stopping. What was on board had to last hundreds of men more than three months.

On Monday July 24th 1837, the *Susan* began loading her human cargo.

The *Hampshire Telegraph* reported:

*The Susan convict ship for Van Diemen's Land is at Spithead and will sail in a few days. On Monday she took on board 160 prisoners from the* York *hulk in this harbour.*

The Register of the *Susan* disclosed that Wainewright was the 76th put aboard, ferried out from the rotting hulk to the ship that was to take him to the other side of the world.

By August 4th, the *Susan* was ready, bearing her full complement of crew, 299 male convicts and an armed guard from the 80th Regiment. Her master, Captain Henry Neatby, who had made the same voyage the previous year, gave the command on the next day and the Susan slipped away down the Solent carrying her cargo of human misery to the civil death to which they'd been consigned.

It cost the Government £20 to sent Wainewright, or any other convict, to Van Diemen's Land, then about £7 a year to keep him there. The cost and the effectiveness of transportation were carefully documented because at the time it seemed an answer to many problems. Sir John Franklin, the Arctic explorer, who himself had been sent to the other end of the world to become lieutenant-governor of Van Diemen's Land in January of 1837, detailed what he called the three great objects of transportation.

The first was "expelling dangerous and mischievous subjects from the body and society at home" and acting as a deterrent to others. Secondly came the reformation of the prisoner and thirdly the physical interests of the colonies – in other words populating the empire, for Van Diemen's Land was both a gaol and a land for free settlers.

The system did give hardened villains a chance to rehabilitate themselves and many found themselves better off; the original of Dickens' Magwitch in *Great Expectations* was said to be worth £40,000 a year in New South Wales through dealings in property and sheep.

But there were also great drawbacks to the system. It lumped together the incurably bad and the potentially reclaimable, though which category Wainewright fitted in is dubious. The assignation of convicts to settlers as servants was, in many cases, virtual slavery and was stopped in 1840 because of abuses.

In 1812 the convict ship *Indefatigable* was the first to take convicts from England to the shores of Van Diemen's Land. The traffic continued until 1853 when the name was changed to Tasmania and transportation there ceased, though it continued elsewhere.

The years between 1831 and 1840 were the high point of the transportation policy. More than 42,000 men and 7,000 women were sent to New South Wales and Van Diemen's Land. So were a large number of boys. Again, crimes against property were fiercely dealt with; in the three years alone between 1827 and 1830, more than 8,500 men and youths were convicted as poachers, and a high proportion of them shipped away in broad-arrowed felt suits, shackles on their ankles.

As the *Susan* was heading to the south Atlantic, at Westminster a select committee of the House of Commons, chaired by Sir William Molesworth, was investigating the whole issue of transportation. The Molesworth report,[1] published the following year, exposed many evils and recommended an end to the system. There was talk of moral corruption, savage mistreatment of the convicts and conflict with the free settlers.

*Every kind of gentle feeling of human nature is constantly outraged by the perpetual*

---

[1] *Report of the Select Committee of the House of Commons on Transportation: together with a letter from the Archbishop of Dublin on the same subject: and notes by Sir William Molesworth.* London. Henry Hooper, 1838

*spectacle of the lash – by the gangs of slaves in irons - by the horrid detail in penal settlements; till the heart of the immigrant is gradually deadened to the sufferings of others, and he becomes at last as cruel as the other gaolers of these vast prisons. The whole system of transportation violates the feelings of the adult, barbarizes the habits and demoralizes the principles of the rising generation, and the result is to use the expression of a public newspaper, 'Sodom and Gomorrah' (chaos, even worse than hell on earth – all loss of morality.*

The numbers did begin to diminish; in the decade from 1841 to 1850 the number transported dropped to 26,000 men and some 6,800 women. But the convict ships sailed on for another 30 years, until 1868, when the *Hougoumont* landed the last 207 men in Western Australia. By that time, more than 160,000 convicts had been landed in Australia since the First Fleet left Britain in 1787 - of these some 75,000 went to Van Diemen's Land. Research into the transportation statistics[2] has shown that 81% were, like Wainewright, transported for crimes against property.

His voyage could not possibly have been as bad as that of those 759 unwilling pioneers. The mortality rate among them was fearful - one in nine died.

But even though these early transports were carrying doctors, conditions on some of them were

---

[2] L.L. Robson. *The Convict Settlers of Australia*, Melbourne University Press. 1965

still grim. The main reason for the poor food and the overcrowding was that the private contractors were not allowed to sell the convicts' services - as they had been when transporting them to America - so there was no incentive to feed them well or guard their health. Many died on the voyages; they were one fewer mouth to feed.

The authorities had framed regulations about the cleaning of prisons below decks and on exercise, but in the early years of transportation, these were frequently ignored.

Scurvy, dysentery and typhus were common in the early days; so were wrecks, due to the inefficiency and drunkenness of the transport officers. Two years before Wainewright's voyage, the convict ships *George III* and the *Neva* had gone down with a loss of more than 250 lives.

An inquiry into the loss of the *George III* disclosed that 26 of the 220 convicts had died *en route* from scurvy and damp conditions. The vessel had leaked, there was a shortage of warm clothing and allowances of sugar, lime juice and medical supplies had been cut back. The ship carried two surgeon-superintendents, but there was little that they could do.

Worse was to follow. As the vessel made her way up the d'Entrecasteaux Channel in Van Diemen's Land, she hit the rock which now bears her name and began to sink. The officers and guards kept large numbers of convicts locked in as the lifeboats were filled and got away.

More than 120 people died, including one woman and three children, though most were convicts trapped behind bars in the lower decks.

Surgeons-superintendent, who had been made dogsbodies by the convict captains in the early days, were much more accountable by the 1830's and reported to the Admiralty directly. They were responsible not only for conducting religious services, maintaining the health of the convicts and crew and inspecting the ventilation and cleanliness of the their quarters, but also but also for rations – seeing that the convicts got enough to eat and that they took daily doses of sugar and lime juice to guard against scurvy.

Sometimes there were tasks beyond the call of duty. John Wilson, surgeon-superintendent of the *Emma Eugenia*, a convict ship carrying 170 women which sailed a few years after the *Susan* reported to his superiors:

> *Jane Grady. This case is marked Dyspepsia in the absence of a more appropriate designation. The patient had had a very irregular life for several years and was nineteen times in jail before Conviction. Her present illness appeared to be the consequence of her jumping overboard halfway between the Cape & Hobart Town. She had handcuffs on at the time as a punishment for striking & wounding the Chief Officer. About fifteen minutes afterwards I caught her by the hair about half-arms length under water.*

The *Susan's* voyage was much less dramatic. There is a detailed record of the voyage and the health of her crew and passengers, kept by Edward Hilditch, the Surgeon-superintendent on board, whose report to the Admiralty is preserved in the National Archives.[3]

Hilditch kept meticulous records of his time aboard the *Susan*, particularly of the treatment of those who became severely ill. He reported that many of the convicts were already sick when they embarked. He gave the hundreds of men a medical check aboard the *Susan* before the voyage began; one was so ill that he was sent directly to hospital on shore and failed to make the journey.

Many prisoners from the hulks were not in good health, Hilditch reported, due to their "innutritious" diet; those from the gaols were better and "nearly all were in good spirits and anxious to proceed.

"The condition of the generality of them improved under the liberal allowances of the Convict Ship and they were landed at Hobart Town in a high state of health".

Reading the report one gets the feeling that Hilditch wanted to please his masters at the Admiralty and rather glossed over the privations of more than three months at sea in a small vessel with more than 300 people on board, nearly half of whom suffered from one ailment or another - seven of them fatally.

In fact according to Hilditch's treatment records, he attended 128 cases on the voyage. Of these he declared that 105 were cured, and that seven died, six convicts and one guard.

The remainder, including Wainewright, ended up in hospital in Hobart.

---

[3] HO11/11

The ailments were mainly "affections of the mucous membranes and of the stomach and bowels". This diarrhoea was most effectively treated with a mixture of chalk and opium.

The most serious complaint, from which several men suffered, was erysipelas, a severe streptococcal infection of the face and scalp, from which died one of the guards, John Hall, who was only 24. Without antibiotics, there was no permanent cure.

Another John Hall, a convict of 26, died of enteritis. Pneumonia did for another two young men; two convicts in their forties were carried off by retention of urine and dyspepsia. Since indigestion is rarely fatal, it seems likely that, as Surgeon Wilson of the *Emma Eugenia* had indicated, dyspepsia was used to describe anything abdominal which could not be diagnosed.

The mortality rate had dropped significantly since the First Fleet set sail and there is argument that the convict transports, despite their great shortcomings, were actually a healthier environment than the rotting hulks in which many spent their lives.

As to the passage itself, reported Hilditch, the weather became oppressive off Madeira when the temperature reached 76 degrees Fahrenheit. Then it became fine with light winds. In this sort of weather, prisoners were allowed to be on deck from sunrise to sundown, being "exercised by dancing, boxing and other similar amusements".

At 7 a.m. the windsails would be put up, which diverted air into the quarters beneath, the scuttles and ventilators were opened and the bedding aired daily on the poop. The prison quarters were kept dry and clean with holystoning – rubbing stones on the decks to remove dirt - and fumigation with chloride of lime. The sick were visited twice a day regularly, and often more frequently during a gale.

Another way of relieving the tedium of the voyage was for the convicts to receive voluntary religious instruction from Peter Barrow, the son of the secretary to the Admiralty, Sir John Barrow. Young Barrow was going to Van Diemen's Land to take up a religious teaching post as a catechist at the Point Puer prison for boys on January 1, 1838.

Separate transport ships were used to bring out boys from Britain on at least eight occasions, the first being Frances Charlotte in 1837, with 140 boys on board. The "young incorrigibles", up to 19 years old, were to learn trades to make them useful members of society.

The vengeful British judges had put boys aboard the *Susan*. Thos. McMahon and Joseph Heaven were both seven years old and there were three 14-year-olds.

Barrow had "made human nature a particular study, especially during his residence on the coast of Africa" and believed all human beings were reclaimable. He was wont to lecture those who would listen on the need for a sober, righteous and godly life. He had some success, claiming that 105 of the prisoners attended his meetings. Records show that Wainewright was not among his pupils.

In the last week of October, the light winds disappeared as the *Susan* rounded the Cape of Good Hope on the 22$^{nd}$ and entered the Roaring Forties, the howling winds and huge seas of the

Southern Ocean. There was to be no respite until they landed a month later.

Hilditch noted: "When in latitude 40 south and longitude 39, to her arrival in Hobart Town, the *Susan* experienced with little intermission a succession of strong westerly gales accompanied by a very heavy sea."

"She was shipping a large quantity of water which frequently floated (sic) the prison deck in spite of the hatches being battened down."

Conditions below decks would have been dire; wet, noisome and dark for weeks on end with the constant shuddering of the hull throwing men about in their cages on the sodden decks beneath.

Bedding would have been saturated. Wainewright came down with rheumatism, diagnosed and noted by Hilditch on November 12.

It was a long, dangerous and uncomfortable trip, but at least it was fast, by the standards of the time. On November 22, 1837, 109 days after clearing the Isle of Wight, the *Susan* approached Hobart Town, the seventh convict ship to arrive there that year.[4]

As the pilot nursed her up the Derwent, a red flag fluttered up the signal staff overlooking Sullivan's Cove in Hobart Town. It meant 'ship from England with male convicts'. The voyage was over, a new life of relentless toil, illness and degradation was beginning.

---

[4] The one before her, the *Platina* took 172 days. In 1842, when she was 29 years old, the *Susan* made the trip in 91 days. The record - Queenstown (Cork) to Hobart Town in 80 days - was set by the *Rodney* in 1853.

Meanwhile in London the costly legal chaos that Wainewright had left behind was to drag on even while he was in serving his sentence in Van Diemen's Land.

Two trials had resolved the issue of the Imperial case in December 1835, but eight years after Helen's death there were still proceedings pending against the Eagle and the Pelican. The Eagle case finally came to trial in June 1838.

This was the case that Henry Smith of the Eagle had tried so hard to prevent - Rush v Peacock. The defendant was Walter Anderson Peacock, a director of the Eagle for more than 40 years and J. L Rush was the administrator of Helen's will, acting on behalf of Madalina, the beneficiary.

The *Morning Herald* report of the case makes it clear that Rush, who had been clerk to Benjamin Wheatley, Madalina's late husband, had been appointed by the Court of Chancery to deal with Helen's will and the law reports of the time specify that this action was taken because although Wainewright the original executor had been granted probate in May 1831, he was now "residing out of the jurisdiction of Her Majesty's courts".

Virtually the same cast of high-cost lawyers who had appeared in the previous two trials appeared before Lord Denman and a special jury in the court of Queen's Bench. The Attorney-general was leading for the Eagle, and Mr Erle for Rush.

Many of the old arguments were reiterated, most particularly that some of the banknotes used to pay the premiums of £300 had been traced directly to Wainewright and that material circumstances had been concealed from the insurers. The Eagle's counsel maintained that Helen had no interest in the policies, which had been effected solely on behalf of Wainewright – the issue which had decided the previous trial in favour of the Imperial.

Lord Denman's summing up was quite neutral. The jury must decide whether Helen really had any interest in the policies, or whether she had ignorantly or fraudulently lent herself to further the purposes of Wainewright.

Whatever the cause of her death, if they found that she had been "sacrificed to his schemes" as he put it, they must find for the Eagle. But the firm would lose if the jury thought the policies had been fairly effected for her own advantage and whether she had borrowed the money from Wainewright to pay for the premiums made no difference.

The jury went out just after 7pm and returned about 90 minutes later with a verdict in favour of the Eagle.

But it still was not over. There were very substantial costs to be paid. Helen's estate consisted of nothing without the insurance money. Her beneficiary and sister Madalina was newly-widowed with three small children.

Mr Erle was back in court in November asking for the verdict to be set aside and permission granted for a new trial. The grounds were a technicality – a clerk who had attested to various statements in the case had not himself been produced in court to swear to them.

Permission was granted, but there was no intention of having a new trial. The ruling was used as a lever against the Eagle. If they would agree not to claim the substantial costs they were due from the previous trial, there would be no further legal action and Madalina would not have to pay the Eagle's costs.

In November 1839, a year later, policy number 80230 on the life of Helen Francis Phoebe Abercromby was finally given back to the Eagle to be cancelled. Eliza and Wainewright's stratagems had, after nine years, come to nothing.

# CHAPTER 20

# BREAKING STONES IN THE CHAIN GANG

*They chain us two by two,
and whip and lash along,
They cut off our provisions if
we do the least thing wrong,
They march us in the burning sun,
until our feet are sore,
So hard's our lot now we are got
upon Van Diemen's shore.*[1]

Van Diemen's Land was discovered in 1642 by the Dutch navigator Abel Tasman and named after his patron, Antony Van Diemen, the Governor-general of the Dutch East Indies. It was made a British colony in 1825 and almost immediately used as a dumping ground for convicts.

No. 2325 Wainewright was taken off the *Susan* two days after she arrived at Sullivan's Cove and sent to the prison hospital with 15 other convicts. The others on board had to wait another three days before being disembarked.

Surgeon Hilditch, whom some have called idle, though his log and the treatment of his patients belies this, sent a note to the Governor of Van Diemen's Land, Sir John Franklin, to announce the

---

[1] Convict ballad printed in the *Launceston Advertiser* 21 November, 1839.

arrival of his cargo and to complain that he himself was suffering from rheumatism so acute that he was unable to come ashore to pay his respects. It was the first convict ship on which he had served, but the experience of the voyage did not deter him, as he made a similar trip in the *Theresa* in 1839.

Wainewright's particulars were noted the day he arrived; they are in the Convicts' Description List now in the Tasmanian Archives:

| | |
|---|---|
| **Name** | **Wainwright (sic) Griffiths Thomas** |
| **Trade** | **Painter** |
| **Height (without shoes)** | **5/5 ½** |
| **Age** | **43** |
| **Complexion** | **Pale** |
| **Head** | **Oval** |
| **Hair** | **Brown** |
| **Whiskers** | **"** |
| **Visage** | **Oval** |
| **Forehead** | **High** |
| **Eyebrows** | **Brown** |
| **Eyes** | **Grey** |
| **Nose** | **Long** |
| **Mouth** | **Large** |
| **Chin** | **Long** |
| **Remarks** | **None** |

He left the hospital five days later on November 27, 1837 and appeared before the Appropriation Authorities, as they were called, who were to determine what to do with him, and noted his replies to their questions:

> *Transported for Forgery. Gaol report not known. Hulk report Good. Married 1 child, stated this offence, Forging a power of Attorney in order that the money which was left to my Wife might come to me. Married one child. Wife Eliza. I have been separated from her for some years.*

It was also noted that he

> "*understands Latin and Greek, has been accustomed to writing for the Journals, first rate Painter in drawings and writing*". (sic)

He was lucky not to be sent to the remote penal institution at Port Arthur, which was notorious for its corporal punishment regime. Many educated convicts were sent there as an extra humiliation because they were considered to have abused their advantages in life. Their dreaded destination is now listed as a UNESCO world heritage site willingly visited by thousands, who can dine in the Felons Restaurant.

Like most prisoners, Wainewright was directed to be employed on the public works around Hobart. Written on his papers were "to be worked on the roads". Could the aesthete and dandy ever have imagined that being shackled and breaking stones in a chain gang would be his fate?

Convict Regulations declared with biblical sonority: "This is a stage through which all must pass and in which the incorrigible must remain even to the termination of his (sic) period of transportation". The chain gang left the Prisoners'

Barracks in Hobart Town at six in the morning. "They are to go out to work in Indian file and no conversation is allowed among them".

Marshalled by an overseer with a stick, they shuffled out of the barracks in their yellow uniforms, holding their hammers in one hand and in the other a piece of twine to prevent their shackles from dragging on the road.

The clinking convoy marched to wherever they were to break stones, which they did all day with an hour's break for "short rations and water" at breakfast, and another hour for dinner. Then came the march back to barracks.

It is clear from the Regulations that the punishment was meant to be harsh:

> *The object... is to teach the convicts habitually to regard as the desert and consequence of guilt the coercive labour they are subjected to ... and that a new course of life alone can lead to their being released from it.*

Floggings were frequent, for indiscipline and malingering, but there was a process of gradual easement for those who behaved themselves - or became too sick to continue the relentless manual labour.

A previous Lieut-governor Sir William Denison had noted in one report that there were 8,000 convicts in custody in 32 work gangs "formed of a debased and sickly class of persons".

Various penal systems were tried. The first involved convicts being assigned to the free settlers as cheap labour, though this led to many abuses and was later abandoned. From the 1840s, there was a probation system whereby the deserving could progress through road gangs and penal stations to be rewarded by a ticket-of-leave that allowed a prisoner to live independently, to work for a wage and perhaps eventually receive a conditional or free pardon and even permission to marry.

At the start of transportation those considered 'gentlemen' were issued immediately with a ticket, but by 1837 rules had changed and a lifer like Wainewright could expect several years of probation before he could be considered.

But piecing together his time in Hobart, he seems to have been breaking stones for some two years before being released from the chain gang. In one of his petitions he wrote: "Two years at the barrow have made sore inroads in a frame always sickly."

The aesthete shuddered at the experience. It had "shaken his reason" having to associate with "men whose language and sentiments startle the oldest London thieves". He pleads elsewhere to the Governor to "grant me the power to shelter my eyes from Vice in her most revolting and sordid phase, and my ears from a jargon of filth & blasphemy".

At the start of 1840, he must have been pleased to be assigned to a slightly more congenial job, as an "invalid wardsman without pay" at the newly-extended Colonial Hospital.

But the hospital in those days was more dreaded than the gaol, wrote James Backhouse Walker in a memoir of the 1840s in Hobart. "It was a convict hospital with bare whitewashed walls, comfortless, evil-smelling and dreary". A report a few years earlier said there were more patients than beds, some were sleeping on the floor, nearly touching each other. "The air from respiration becomes speedily vitiated and the exhalations from the bodies in a morbid state so highly condensed as to prove not only noxious to themselves but injurious to the public".

This hospital and a few other primitive medical facilities looked after huge numbers of people. Apart from the convicts themselves, there was the civilian and military population, which included six regiments of the line. By the 1840s there were also some 10,000 emancipists, convicts who had served their sentences, and about 30,000 free settlers "the labouring poor" as they were called.

Labouring but not worthy, according to the historian of Hobart hospital, who described them as "ill-educated grasping colonials given to excessive drinking and brutality".

Violence was a commonplace, but worse was disease, which was rife in the colony. There were frequent outbreaks of influenza and one strange episode in which dozens of dogs died in the streets from distemper. In 1840 there was an epidemic of what was called a "typhoid-like fever". More than 900 people were affected, almost all of them convicts and 82 of them died as the disease rampaged through the population for seven weeks. It was highly- infectious; 95 out of a convict road gang of 120 went down with it.

The convict hospital was full to overflowing and in one day 22 seriously-ill convicts had to be turned away as there was no room for them. The *Colonial Times* trumpeted on March 3, 1840: "The hospital, far from being a clean and airy place for treatment, is the very focus of infection". In this "nest of uncleanliness", as the newspaper called it, laboured Wainewright. He was extraordinary lucky. Twelve of the convict attendants died.

Two years later, scarlet fever arrived from Sydney and was endemic in the colony for many years. In this 1842 epidemic, 23 people died; another 41 died the following year. The staff sometimes ventured on operations - the hospital records show dozens between 1840-1859, almost all of them were the most basic of procedures, amputations of the limbs.

Shortly after arriving at the hospital and although he was only three years into his life sentence in 1840, Wainewright took the bold step of short-circuiting the convict authorities, who would not have granted him any form of cessation for a number of years, and applied directly to London to Lord Normanby, the Colonial Secretary, for a free pardon.

The petition[2], discovered in the National Archives, has never been published before and can be found in full in Appendix 2. The document is marked "Presented by Mr T. Von Holst, Nassau Street, and Middlesex Hospital". Holst, was of course, Wainewright's artist friend who gave him shelter when he returned from Francc.

In essence it says that he wants to return to France where he is appreciated, because "in England, though pardoned, he would be ever excluded from the Society of Gentlemen". However, he then goes on to list all the well-known figures with whom he was associated as evidence of his superior background.

---

[2] National Archives HO17/101

There's a long rambling section about collecting materials for a psychological work on the *Analogies of the Imagination*. The most interesting part of the petition deals with his crime, repeating the claim that he had been tricked into confessing because he had been promised leniency, but then drags Eliza into it - "his Wife consenting and aiding, as the forged Power manifests". It does no such thing, as the forgeries were in his own hand. However, this is the first, but not the last time that Eliza is to be blamed.

"Have pity," he implores Lord Normanby, "on a mind nearly strangled but worthy perhaps of life and remember that you Word has the potency of a God. Life or Death hangs on your decision", he concludes melodramatically.

The Secretary of State was not inclined to pity. The application was refused despite a remarkable testimonial which was attached to it. It was written by Dr Edward Bedford, assistant surgeon at the Colonial Hospital and dated 27 October 1840:

> *I have had the opportunity of watching the character and conduct of the petitioner from his arrival in this colony and more particularly since he has been in my service.*
>
> *He has always conducted himself with great propriety.*
>
> *His sufferings have been great and his mind had received a great shock from his distress.*
>
> *I most strongly recommend his petition to Your Lordship's most favourable consideration.*

It is likely that Dr Bedford had discovered Wainewright's artistic talents and had used him to make anatomical drawings, something another transported artist Thomas Bock was said to have done.[3]

Dr Bedford was the son of the senior chaplain to the colony, the Rev William Bedford, known to the convicts as Holy Willie because of his excoriation of sinners. Wainewright sketched not only Holy Willie, but also the doctor's two daughters.

The doctor seems to have been as strong-willed as his father and fell out with the establishment at the Colonial Hospital. His contract to look after the hospital, the penitentiary and the Sandy Bay road gang was ended and he opened his own hospital, St Mary's, in Campbell Street, Hobart, in 1841, dedicated to serving the "labouring classes" . The archives office of Tasmania suggests that Dr Bedford employed Wainewright there as a medical orderly.

What Dr Bedford's testimonial does show is that Wainewright was physically feeble and in a fragile state of mind; it also calls into question all the horror stories of his conduct in the colony which were to emerge from Victorian writers in their frequent fits of morality.

---

[3] Bock, who was from Birmingham, was a talented miniaturist and engraver, sent to Van Diemen's Land in 1823 for giving a woman drugs to induce an abortion; he became a fashionable painter in the colony and engraved its first banknotes.

## CHAPTER 21

## ARTIST *REDIVIVUS*

It is ironic that Wainewright did his best work in captivity as a broken man in both mind and body, almost the stereotype of the tortured artist whose greatest gifts are stimulated by physical pain and mental anguish, art and suffering intertwined. He was now both orderly and patient at the Colonial Hospital after his spell with Dr Bedford at St Mary's.

He had been admitted in 1842 with "bodily weakness such as to effectually prevent his being employed by the Government in any kind of laborious occupation". He was said by the staff surgeon, Dr Mair, to have an "enfeebled state of the system generally and a peculiar proneness to gastric and nervous irritation".

When he was not carrying out his menial tasks around the wards at the Colonial Hospital he was portraying Hobart's middle classes for he had become well-known for his talents by the administrative and medical staff he encountered at the hospital who had spread news among their friends about his abilities.

He became a portraitist, executing likenesses of the officials and their families, some done for small sums, others for favours which had been granted to him. The lovely picture of Jane and Lucy Cutmear was done for their father, who was the gatekeeper at the hospital and kept Wainewright supplied with artists' materials.

# THE FATAL CUP

The charming Cutmear twins, Jane and Lucy, at about nine years old, depicted in pencil and watercolour, were the daughters of the gatekeeper at the hospital where Wainewright worked. Lucy is the one with the kiss-curl. One critic has described this picture as 'a masterpiece of delicacy'.
*Now in the Australian National Gallery*

The pencil and wash drawing was done around 1842, when they were eight or nine years old. Like many of Wainewright's drawings, the detail is all in the face and hair. Alas, the twins did not live long. Lucy, the one with the curl, died some two years later and her sister when she was 21.

Joanna Gilmour, curator of the National Portrait Gallery in Canberra, describes Wainewright's his works as being among the finest examples of colonial portraiture, noted for their charm, skill and delicacy as well as for the faces of Hobart society they document.[1]

She estimates that he created portraits for about 56 sitters, some of them influential figures in the colony such as the Lieutenant-governor Sir John Franklin (who was removed from office in 1843), the entrepreneur Edward Lord and the Surveyor-general Robert Power. About 40 of the portraits are known to exist.

One of the most striking is the watercolour of Dr Frederick John Clarke, the surgeon at the Colonial Hospital, for whom Wainewright worked and who furnished him with testimonials for his appeals. There were at least four versions of this picture.

Wainewright also painted at least two watercolours which would have been considered erotica at the time, *Lothaire of Bourgogne Discovers the Amour of his Wife with the High Constable* and the *Reunion of Eros and Psyche*. They both came up for auction in Australia in 2001. They had originally been acquired by Dr Robert Kennedy

---

[1] *Portrait* magazine, January 2013. National Portrait Gallery, Canberra.

# THE FATAL CUP

Dr Robert Kennedy Nuttall came to Van Diemen's Land as assistant surgeon to his brother-in-law Dr Clarke. He was to see Wainewright at the hospital almost every day for several years and collected many of his works including the self-portrait. Dr Nuttall's son George became a distinguished biologist and Cambridge professor.

Nuttall, an assistant surgeon at the hospital and Dr Clarke's brother-in-law, whose family held several of Wainewright's works for many years.

Wainewright not only painted Nuttall himself but sketched on the back of one of the surgeon's report forms, his own self-portrait with the ironic caption: *"Head of a Convict, very characteristic of low cunning & revenge!*

Many of these pictures came back to England with the Nuttall family, though some were said to have been lost during the Second World War. The family kindly showed me those that remained and let me photograph them at their home in Surrey many years ago.

Wainewright had painted in London, long before his deportation, three of the Foss family - Edward, whose signature he had forged, his brother Henry and sister Fanny. All three pictures were thought to have been lost, but that of Edward reappeared recently. It had been in the Foss family until 2014, when it was auctioned at Bonhams in Sydney. It sold for AU$103,700, some £60,000.

Other works are held by the National Gallery of Australia in Canberra, the Art Gallery of South Australia in Adelaide and the Tasmanian Museum and Art Gallery in Hobart.

In April 1844, Wainewright petitioned yet another Lieutenant-governor of Van Diemen's Land, Sir John Eardley-Wilmot, for a ticket-of-leave, one of the many steps towards redemption in the strict probation system of the penal colonies, described by the Australian writer Robert Hughes as being like a game of snakes and ladders. The ticket-of-leave would allow him freedom in which he could

Dr Frederick John Clarke was the Colonial Surgeon at Hobart. This watercolour was one of at least four of him that Wainewright produced. Dr Clarke put forward Wainewright's application for a ticket-of-leave saying that it would improve his health and allow him "to "use his superior talents as an artist".

work for himself, provided he remained in Hobart and reported regularly to the local authorities. He was supposed to go to church on Sundays.

The petition (Appendix 3) is preserved in the Mitchell Library, Sydney, and shows the pathetic state into which Wainewright had sunk. There is a long confused recital of his ancestry, his schooling, accounts of people he knew, books he had written but never had published, and other accomplishments, none of which is relevant to the appeal.

What is more interesting is his declaration of "entire Innocence" of the bank fraud for which he was transported; he repeats that it was his money after all, but then goes on to say that he admits knowledge of the actual committer, but "such however were their relative positions that to have disclosed it would have made him infamous where any human feeling is manifest".

In other words he is blaming Eliza for the forgeries - she had made him do it even though it was he who went to the Bank of England with the forged signatures on the powers of attorney in his own hand, and he who withdrew the cash, taking the huge risk of being hanged if he was found out at the time. In his previous petition for a free pardon four years before, he maintained that Eliza was "consenting and aiding" in the crime; now he was saying she was the 'committer' - the inference being that he was merely her puppet..

Such was the extent of Wainewright's sense of grievance that for more than two decades he was resentful about his sentence, which he always considered wrongful, and his treatment at the Old Bailey which had led to his transportation, rather

# THE FATAL CUP

The graceful watercolour, gouache and pencil portrait of Martha Sarah Butler, wife of a Hobart lawyer. The brooch and drop earring details are important, as she was known for her love of jewellery; her maiden name was Asprey, the same as that of the famous London jewellers. She is said to have lost the collection she brought from London when her ship was wrecked as it approached Hobart. Wainewright also drew f her husband and their three daughters.
*National Portrait Gallery Canberra*

than being grateful for the fact that the authorities had allowed him to escape the hangman's noose and a public execution.

His petition went first to the police office for checks on his behaviour in the colony and was then forwarded to the governor's office. Attached to the petition was a summary which said that he had never been charged with any misconduct, and a medical opinion from Dr Clarke at the hospital where Wainewright had been a patient for two and a half years which said that "it would ameliorate his bodily ailments if his mind could be relieved by the extension to him of some Indulgence." Testimonials about his good behaviour were attached.

Despite the encomia, the application for the ticket-of-leave was refused. Lieut-governor Eardley-Wilmot, soon to be recalled to London for incompetence, scrawled across it "A TL wd be contrary to Act of Parlt. TL refused".

It was rejected on May 16, 1844, because he had not served enough of his sentence to qualify under the strict probation rules. But indulgence was granted two weeks later when he was given a third class Probation Pass, which allowed him a little more freedom. Eventually the much-desired ticket-of-leave was granted in December 1845 and a year later a conditional pardon.

At the time the colony was suffering from an economic depression. There had been a large influx of convicts after Britain ended transportation to New South Wales, in 1842 alone more than 5,300 arrived. Many ticket-of-leave convicts could not find work and thousands of former prisoners

# THE FATAL CUP

Wainewright's portraits, drawn and painted for favours and small sums, unsurprisingly tended to flatter their sitters, the women looking winsome and the men distinguished. This sitter here is unknown.

became dependent on the government, leading to the collapse of the probation system.

Wainewright, though had special talents and was free to charge a few shillings a day for his portraiture and live where he pleased. Reminiscences of the time record him as shuffling around Hobart in a long blue coat and peaked cap, chewing sticks of opium, an unremarkable habit at the time when the British empire traded in opium, drugs laws were non-existent and his former Romantic acquaintances, de Quincy and Coleridge had been addicted to it because of its effect in distorting time and space. But it seems it had not reduced him to the "putrefying dunghill" that was Coleridge, according to Thomas Carlyle.

It is likely that Wainewright had been treated as an out-patient at the hospital where he worked, as prisoners without the necessary indulgences had still to be confined in the Prisoners' Barracks, but being free, he now moved to lodgings in 8, Campbell Street, a stone's throw from the barracks and hospital.

We know this because the owners of the lodgings, a Mr M'Donald put a notice in the Colonial Times in December 1846:

*If Mr Thomas Griffiths Wainewright does not fetch away his Books and Goods left in my house, the same will be sold by me on account of money due to me for his lodging and other matters.*

Indebted to the end, which was now near, for he was now back in the hospital after suffering a stroke in which he lost the use of one of his hands. On Sunday, August 17th, 1847 he had another massive stroke which killed him. His 10-year long ordeal was over.

Jonathan Curling's 1938 biography quotes a letter written by Agnes Power, wife of the Surveyor-general from her home in Derwentwater south of Hobart, to her daughter Ellen in England:

> ...*Bye the bye, the unfortunate Wainewright is dead - he died this day week of apoplexy. He had been a long time very ill, had lost the use of his hand and was altogether in a miserable state of poverty as well as illness, and had gone to the Hospital... He certainly was a wonderful man, full of talent and fuller still of wickedness. The last time I ever saw him before, he said all he wished for was to go home and murder the person who had transported him - of course I affected to think he was jesting, but I am quite sure he was in earnest.*

Had he meant it, there were several candidates. The most likely would have been his relative Edward Foss who discovered the forgeries and set the pursuit in motion, then there was Mr Cope the governor of Newgate who persuaded him to plead guilty, the judge who sentenced him, the Home Secretary who had not considered his last desperate appeal...

"Perhaps no blacker soul ever passed from a body than passed the day Wainewright went to his account", declared Walter Thornbury melodramatically. Where his body lies is not known.

In copper-plate writing on the still-preserved record of Convict 2325 is the word *Dead*. The capital *D* is nearly two inches high.

## CHAPTER 22

## ELIZA'S PLIGHT

*"It would have to be regretted if this lady should die from starvation."*

Eliza, living in London in desperate straits, was not to hear of his death for months. The chaos he had left behind by defrauding the Bank of England had to be sorted out. The Bank had been tricked, the money had been wasted away, now the loss had to be made good.

Edward Foss, whose name had been forged was now the chief trustee of the settlement, and a man of great probity and resolution, wrote to the Bank's chief accountant in May 1835 - five months after the theft had been discovered - and demanded the replacement of the stock.

Freshfields replied that the Bank admitted liability but they would be entitled to Wainewright's life interest in the dividends and would replace the stock therefore on his death. Foss didn't agree; it might put him, as a trustee, in an awkward position in years to come when Wainewright's family called on him for the money. He put the case to counsel, Edward Jacob of Lincolns Inn who concurred. The stock should be replaced in the names of the trustees at once.

Then as the long wrangle began between the Bank and Foss, he received a letter from Eliza, now separated from her husband for four and a half years. She was destitute and fearing starvation for herself and the workhouse for young Griffiths. But she had not forgotten the marriage settlement of 18 years before, and Foss, she thought, could help her.

She wrote from the small house in Fulham to which she had moved after Helen's death.

*July 3/35*           *9 Markham Place*
*King's Road*
*Dear Sir,*
*Will you permit me to engage your attention for a few minutes. My utter destitution, for I have vainly endeavoured to obtain a livelihood, allows to my friends who cannot otherwise assist me the privilege of give advice. In consequence I am strongly pressed to obtain the restitution of my Settlement.*

*It is true the daily prospect of starvation, or the worse horror of condemning my nice promising boy to a workhouse (when he is entitled to an income, which though moderate, yet is sufficient to warrant a good education) would stimulate me to try much but this does not appear to me feasible and I have resolved in my own mind to depend on no advice but yours if I can be so fortunate to obtain it.*

*I trust you will not think me impertinent in this quest, I do not mean to be so, but my mind is so bewildered by increasing distress that I fear I cannot rightly judge between right and wrong.*

*I am, Dear Sir, Your much obliged*
*E.F. Wainewright.*

It's ironic that she should write that she could not distinguish between right and wrong given the catalogue of felony with which she had been involved.

Foss replied a month later. He was sorry, but because of the "peculiar circumstances" in which he was placed, he could not interfere or give advice.

But unknown to Eliza, he did intervene, sending her letter to the Bank with another request that there should be no further delay in replacing the stock. His motive was not, at this time, altruistic; he wanted to use Eliza as a lever, his problem was legalistic - she could help him unwittingly to satisfy the terms of his trusteeship.

In August he tried again to get the fund restored. Freshfields fended him off. "I think", they wrote to him, "you are acting with very unnecessary strictness to the injury of the Bank without any advantage to anyone."

Foss made a further attempt the following February, and again his plea met with obfuscation. By October his patience had run out. He wrote sternly: "Unless the stock shall be transferred within the next seven days I shall feel it my duty to proceed."

Freshfields were impelled into some sort of action. "There are certain forms to be gone through", they replied, "which preclude this question from being disposed of in seven days, but in the course of the next week, I hope to be authorised to come to you on the subject."

On the same day the solicitors notified the Bank formally that the stock should be replaced and the dividends held by the Bank during Wainewright's life. It had not been replaced so far they said, because of the high price of stock, but now the trustees were threatening proceedings.

The Court and Directors of the Bank agreed; the deed was drawn up. Foss, who had won a fight, but not the battle, refused to accept the offer. The stock, he insisted, must be in the trustees' name, not the Bank's.

Now the legal infighting really started. Relations between the two sides became frosty. Said Freshfields: "I have a strong feeling that if the Bank are compelled to look at the case with the strictness the trustees seem disposed to exercise, they might resist the claim *in toto.*"

Foss was not to be intimidated. "I do not like to see the last claim in your letter. It seems to convey a sort of threat". He put the case again before counsel, and again counsel agreed: the trustees were fully entitled to have the stock in their names.

Another six months passed. Wainewright appeared at the Old Bailey and was transported. Foss tried again. "The offender having been brought to justice renders it more necessary that no further delay should take place." The Bank could delay no longer. Two and a half years after the loss was discovered, the stock was finally replaced in the names of the trustees.

Relations between the two solicitors became cordial; the Bank paid Foss's expenses and even added ten guineas "for his trouble", which perhaps, was the least they could do.

Although Foss's sense of legal propriety might have been satisfied, Eliza was still in trouble. But now that her husband had been transported there was a slight hope; she was surely entitled to the dividends under the marriage settlement now that he was in a state of *civiliter mortuus* - civil death – the loss of all civil rights because of his conviction as a felon.

Madalina put her in touch with her own lawyer, Mr W.H. Frampton of Grays Inn, who had tried to bring the case against the Eagle. Frampton promised to do what he could, but Foss soon got to hear of it and gave the Bank a warning and a piece of gratuitous advice. "He is trying to get the dividends for Mrs Wainewright. I do not think he has a leg to stand on." Foss may well have been a lot more suspicious of what Eliza had done than her sister Madalina.

Two years passed. Griffiths was now 11, had been farmed out and didn't know whether his father was alive or dead. Eliza's plight grew more desperate. In March 1839 she saw only one recourse, a petition to the Queen to attempt to get some of the settlement paid. She wrote, or rather Frampton wrote for her:

> *Your petitioner is in a destitute situation having no means of support and her infant child is equally destitute and is for the present placed out at a small school in a distant part of the country from your petitioner's residence on casual charity which may at any moment be withdrawn.*

The petition was addressed to the Queen only nominally; its destination was the Treasury, the masters of the Bank of England.

Eliza wanted a certificate every half year to declare that Wainewright was alive and another on his death, which would then liberate the settlement for her. But, in the meantime, she wanted the Treasury to tell Foss to pay her the dividends. They were worth, after all, £260 a year, which would keep her very comfortably.

Frampton sent a covering note with the petition, with the curious submission that the virtual abolition of the death penalty for forging powers of attorney had robbed Eliza and Griffiths of their rightful income. "If he (Wainewright) had met with an untimely end, the unfortunate wife and child, although lamenting the unhappy exit of their protector, would have been differently placed from a pecuniary point of view." In other words they would have got the money is he had been hanged for his crimes.

Foss didn't see how the Treasury could interfere. The Bank's solicitors agreed. They noted: "It is an idle and foolish application and the best way will be to take no further notice." But the problem of Eliza would not quietly go away. Frampton was not going to ignore her poverty nor would he let the Bank do so. His next move was to see the Treasury solicitor, Mr Maule - by coincidence the same lawyer who had prosecuted Wainewright at the Old Bailey.

Maule was willing to help Eliza - but only if the Bank were not opposed to his doing so; and opposed they were. Frampton put on the pressure. He judged that the Bank would be shamed if the poverty-stricken Eliza were to bring an action and he lost no time in telling them so. "I urge the Bank not to drive her to seek relief *in forma pauperis*[1] 'from such gigantic powers as the Crown and the Bank".

He went on to give harrowing details:

> *In a letter I received from her this morning she states that for weeks by, she has had only bread and potatoes to live on; that she is extremely ill; that a too-frequent deprivation of food has induced a paralysis which is often difficult to surmount and only a few days since, whilst in this situation, a ruffian entered and seized some articles of furniture for which she was unable to pay.*

The Bank were not moved by this catalogue of woe. A crime had been committed against property - suffering as a result of it was a seemly thing.

They replied promptly to Frampton:

> *The situation of Mrs Wainewright is much to be deplored, but she has no cause to look to the Bank of England. The Bank have been severe sufferers by the misconduct of Mr Wainewright and we are satisfied that the Crown will not lend itself to the attempt to plunder it further, for such we must regard your threats.*

The Bank were very sensitive about losses, for 10 years previously they had nearly collapsed. The Bank of England was then not like today's

---

[1.] In the form of a pauper - a legal device in which a court can grant someone with no money the right to pursue a case without having to pay costs.

central bank, an arm of government, but a profit-making organisation responsible not only to the government of the day but also to shareholders and other banks. Unwise investments led to a national banking crisis in which the Bank itself nearly went under and 70 other banks collapsed.

But to Frampton's credit - for there can have been no assurance that he was ever going to be paid for all his efforts - he tried one last throw; an appeal strictly on the grounds of mercy:

*The destitute situation of this poor unfortunate woman induces me again to request whether the Bank may not do something for her on her understanding to repay out of income when she should come Into possession. It would have to be regretted if this lady should die from starvation, which is not improbable from her account, that these dividends should have been held by the Bank.*

Foss relented on behalf of the trustees. An income of £50 or £60 a year, he thought, would solve her problems.

On June 20, 1839, the Bank's Court of Directors agreed to allow Eliza £50 a year. The terms they left to Freshfields, who, though paying her £25 at once, imposed an interest rate of five per cent (a half of one per cent below Bank rate) on the sum until Wainewright's death.

Eliza was "very thankful and highly gratified" the directors were told.

After four years of battling with the Bank she was to get less than a pound a week. She was poor, she was ill and she was without a husband. The lavish living of Great Marlborough Street and Linden House were a dream of long ago. And her troubles were still not over. There was to be still more battling with the authorities before she had her due in the settlement.

On Wainewright's death, Eliza became entitled to the dividends from the settlement, but she had to produce a certificate of his death to the Bank of England, and due to a lapse, it was not forwarded to the authorities in England. This was because he was not on the general muster of convicts at the time of his death, but a ticket-of-leave man.

Edward Foss had been told of the death in February 1849 and notified Freshfield's: "I have heard of the kindness of the Directors, towards Mrs Wainewright, but as she is incompetent from ill-health to earn anything and her son is living upon her being now out of employment, it will be evident how impossible it is for them to exist upon the Bank allowance of £50."

The Bank was being asked to loan them money, to be repaid on the certification of Wainewright's death. But certificate came there none, neither it seems, was there a loan from the Bank.

Eliza had heard of the death from the family living in England of Robert Power, the Surveyor-general in Hobart. She had written several letters to the Convict Department and to the Colonial Secretary in Hobart Town attempting to get the death certificate without getting any reply.

In desperation she wrote in February 1849 from her new address in Palace New Road, Lambeth, to the Secretary of State for the Colonies, Earl Grey, he of tea fame, outlining the facts and making her appeal:

*My Lord, I beseech you to shorten the suffering I have so long endured and condescend to expedite the receipt of the necessary Document...the official communication can be obtained by your command.*

She asked for the certificate to be sent to Foss's office on Pall Mall. The civil service lurched into action. The request would have taken three months or so to reach Hobart and another three months for the certificate to reach England, not counting the natural delays of bureaucracy .
Eventually, in August 1849, two years after Wainewright's death, a copy was made of his death certificate:

*Van Diemen's Land*

*I hereby certify that Thomas Griffiths Wainewright, who was tried at the Central Criminal Court on 3rd July 1847 (sic) for Forgery and sentenced to Transportation for Life, under which sentence he arrived at Van Diemen's Land per Susan on 21 November 1837 – died in Her Majestys (sic) General Hospital at Hobart Town on the 17th August 1847.*

*James Thomson*

*Registrar
Convict Department
23 August 1849*

Finally Eliza became entitled to an income from the settlement. In a few months, her life and that of Griffiths were to change dramatically.

## CHAPTER 23

## THE TWO FACES OF JANUS

Janus, the two-faced Roman god, had been Wainewright's pseudonym in his literary days and there were two different faces by which he was represented to the world.

Wild stories about his life in Van Diemen's Land abounded, even before his death. Colnaghi the print-sellers wrote to the Victorian novelist and politician Edward Bulwer Lytton in January 1847: "We have reason to believe that Wainewright has terminated his existence. In attempting to escape he was shot by the sentinel and shortly afterwards expired". This was a complete fiction, as by that time Wainewright had been granted a conditional pardon and was living outside the prison barracks.

Lytton, who is scarcely read today, was a master of purple prose. His 1830 melodrama *Paul Clifford*, begins with the famous cliché: "It was a dark and stormy night..." He would not be pleased to know that he is remembered today in the annual Bulwer Lytton fiction contest in which entrants vie to compose bad opening sentences to imaginary novels.

He would be more gratified to know that his phrase 'the pen is mightier than the sword' from his historical play *Cardinal Richelieu*, is so often quoted, as is "the great unwashed", presumable those who lived outside the bounds of his enormous stately home at Knebworth House in Hertfordshire.

His place in the Wainewright saga comes from his 1846 novel *Lucretia; or the Children of the Night*,[1] in which the character of the artist Gabriel Varney is modelled on the still-living Wainewright; Varney forges a signature to get money from the Bank of England, is tried and transported. Lucretia Clavering, his partner, who is involved in a series of poisonings, is named after Lucretia Borgia and the village of Clavering in Essex which housed the real serial poisoner Sarah Chesham, who became known as Arsenic Sally.

Lytton wrote in the preface to the first edition of *Lucretia*: "The crimes herein related took place within the last 17 years." This handily takes in 1830 when Helen was killed. He went on: "There has been no exaggeration as to their extent, no great departure from their details... I narrate a history, not invent a fiction."

It is significant therefore that the poisoner is not the transported forger but his partner. The poison she used was said to have "baffled every known and positive test in the posthumous examination of surgeons".

---

[1.] Lucretia was a best-seller, but its gory details caused a furore. The Times called it "a disgrace to the writer, a shame to us all." Dr Alfred Swaine Taylor, the toxicologist and Professor of Medical Jurisprudence at Guy's Hospital in London, attacked the book because "the entire plot details and moral form a most complete revelation of the art of murder by poison". Stung by the criticism, Lytton wrote in the preface to the second edition: "The story might have been improved in itself, and rendered more acceptable to the reader, by diminishing the gloom of the catastrophe. In this edition I have endeavoured to do so."

Lucretia is almost certainly Eliza, though Lytton denied this, possibly knowing that she was still alive and that even as a pauper could sue for defamation, having never been charged with any crime. However his grandson, in reminiscences of Lytton's life, said the character was indeed modelled on Eliza.

Lytton was helped in his writing by being given all Wainewright's papers and other possessions which he had left behind in France. They were sent to him by Henry Smith of the Eagle, who had recovered them from Boulogne and Paris, and was greatly flattered by the attentions of the famous author.

"Pray keep the papers until we meet" wrote Smith "they will be the heads on which I can speak.... without my connecting information the papers tell no tale whatsoever."

They had dinner together and on May 26th, 1846, Smith wrote to Lytton:[2]

> *On making a further search, I found a list of the contents of the forfeit trunks, and this led me to a second packet of papers and books which had escaped my first enquiries. I send them to you, and also our schedule made on the strangely assorted cargo coming into our keeping. (You will see your own* Letter to a Cabinet Minister[3] *was retained among his later treasures.) It will show the books which*

---

[2] Smith's correspondence is preserved in the Lytton archive in the Hertfordshire Record Office. D/EK 026280

[3] *A Letter to a late Cabinet Minister on the Present Crisis.* Lytton 1834

225

> *the combination of his necessities and his tastes had left to him amid the general wreck. The drawings come out better than my memory had traced them to you.*
>
> *There is no proof of the nature of the poison used, but the general medical opinion of the time pronounced it to be strychnine. . . . Mr Thompson tells me that W. confessed that he employed strychnine and morphine, and you will gather more of his history from the additional briefs and their notes, now sent to you.*

Thompson had been employed by the Eagle to keep an eye on Wainewright in France. His assertion that Wainewright had confessed to poisoning was hearsay and the only one that was ever made and it is clear from the Smith letters that nothing incriminating was discovered in the trunks. None of Wainewright's possessions has ever been found.

After Wainewright's death Smith wrote again to Lytton on May 2, 1849:

> *His later days in the sick ward were employed I am told in blasphemy to the pious patriarchs and terrifying the timid. I think that he never lived to know the everlasting fame to which he has been damned in* Lucretia.

Damned he was to be in almost everything that was subsequently written about him, in a torrent of vituperation from those he had counted as friends and from Victorian moralisers.

The tone was set by *The Last Glimpse of an Accomplished Scoundrel*, published in the

Melbourne *Spectator* in July 1866, which is worth quoting in full for its unrestrained ferocity in its description of Wainewright:

*A man with a massive head, in which the animal propensities were largely developed, and with a great volume of brain. His eyes were deeply set in his head, he had a square solid jaw, wore his hair long, stooped somewhat and had a snake-like expression, which was both repulsive and fascinating. His conversation and manner were winning in the extreme. He was not intemperate, but grossly sensual; with the intellect of a Pericles and the passions of a satyr. He used to take a dram of opium every day; and it was to procure this indulgence, that he practised painting. If commissioned to execute the portrait of a lady, he would always endeavour to give an erotic direction to the conversation; so that whatever admiration was felt for his genius, was neutralised by the fear and antipathy excited by his lewdness.*

*The malignancy of his character seems to have been ingrained and ineradicable, and he took a perverse pleasure in traducing his benefactors. The only living creature for which he felt affection was a cat, to which he was much attached. Was there a secret affinity between his own nature and that of his pet? Both could boast of the patte des velours[4] and both had a good deal of the tiger in their composition.*

---

[4] Literally velvet paws, colloquially to be charming but disguise one's true feelings.

*He endeavoured to poison two people in Hobart Town who had become obnoxious to him; and no compunctious visitings of conscience ever interfered with the execution of any fell purpose on which he had resolved. One illustration of the savage malignity of his character will serve to show that we have not exaggerated its innate cruelty and depravity.*

*While he was an inmate of the hospital, a patient entered against whom he entertained a grudge. Wainewright's educated and penetrating eye detected the presage of death in the poor fellow's face, and approaching him, he hissed into his ear with venomous earnestness:-'You are a dead man. In four and twenty hours your soul will lie in hell, and my arm will be buried so deep' - touching his elbow – 'dissecting it'.*

This extraordinary concoction, which helped to increase the lurid tide of obloquy, was written nearly 20 years after Wainewright's death, and said to be based on the recollections of Dr. William Crooke, a surgeon at the hospital in Hobart.

It appears to be almost entirely false and fails to mention that Dr Crooke was one of the five hospital staff who had written testimonials of Wainewright's good behaviour to support his petition for a ticket-of-leave, all of them commenting on the fact that no complaint had ever been made about him. There was certainly no evidence of his trying to poison two people.

As to the physical description, rather than having a massive head, a square jaw and snake-like eyes, his own self-portrait shows a rather different and sensitive face. One of the few things which might have been correct was his love of a cat. He had written in his essays of his affection for his dogs and cats and for his chaise horse Contributor.

Another traducer was Dickens' biographer John Forster. He could not conceal his contempt for...

> *the gaudy, violent, flaring artist; the insolent, bullying double-voiced critic; the profane and extravagant entertainer; the shabby cheat; the swindler and forger; the unscrupulous and unsparing murderer; and to the last even when loaded with a felon's chains, the daring and impudent braggart.*

De Quincey, in his essay on Charles Lamb, recalled meeting Wainewright in November 1821:

> *The dinner was memorable by means of one fact not discovered until many years later. Amongst the company, all literary men, sate (sic) a murderer, and a murderer of a freezing class; cool, calculating, wholesale in his operations, and moving all along under the advantages of unsuspecting domestic confidence and domestic opportunities.*

Wainewright became a pantomime villain, one of those Awful Warnings beloved by the Victorians to show how one who was well-bred and well-educated, but suspiciously artistic, could sink to the depth of depravity. Walter Thornbury's 1870 Old *Stories Re-Told* has the fiendish artist-turned-murderer wearing a ring with a secret compartment containing strychnine, which he tips into the drink of his unsuspecting victim during his stay in France. You can almost hear the cries of "he's behind you!"

Walter Allen's 1894 potboiler *Twelve Bad Men*, which is generally fair to Wainewright, if inaccurate, has Forster saying of a picture Wainewright did of a young girl, which was shown at a party in London in 1847 by Lady Blessington, that he had "contrived somehow to put the expression of his own wickedness into the portrait of a nice kind-hearted girl".

None of the existing portraits shows any such malignity, but rather a grace and tenderness; they were, after all, pen and wash drawings which probably flattered the sitters, commissioned by the middle classes of Hobart of themselves and their families, or dashed off for someone who had done him a favour.

Then there is Dickens, who, with Forster, had spotted the imprisoned Wainewright awaiting trial on their visit to Newgate in June 1837. More than 20 years later, his short story *Hunted Down*, had obvious parallels to the Wainewright case. The evil Julius Slinkton is involved in insurance fraud and the death of a young girl. Dickens is also thought to have used Wainewright as the basis for the character of the murderer Blandois in *Little Dorrit*.

Oscar Wilde was kinder to Wainewright suggesting the usefulness of sin in the creation of artistic personality, "His crimes seem to have had an important effect upon his art. They gave a strong personality to his style, a quality that his early work certainly lacked", he declared in 1889 in his essay *Pen, pencil and poison*, concluding: "To be suggestive for fiction is to be of more importance than a fact".

Perhaps the most fanciful examples of the fictional Wainewright come from Australia. In 1961, there was the *Tilted Cross*, a novel by Hal Porter, set in Wainewright's time in Hobart Town, whose main character is a transported forger and suspected poisoner with the clunkingly obvious name of Judas Griffin Vaneleigh.

There is a fascinating alternative tale of Wainewright's exile in France. A book published in Sydney in 1974 by Tom Kenny was entitled *Thomas Griffiths Wainewright in New South Wales*. It claimed that during his absence from London after the death of Helen, he was really in Australia. Not only did he live in New South Wales under various aliases, he also visited Van Diemen's Land several times.

He would then of course have found it quite familiar when he was transported there a few years later. Alas, what evidence is put forward to support this interesting case is based on surmise and conspiracy theory, with no documentation apparently available.

Neither is there any evidence to support other of Kenny's books. One suggests that Wainewright wrote and published the *Pickwick Papers* in Australia, which were then pirated by Dickens. Then there is another in which it is disclosed that Miss Havisham from *Great Expectations* was a solicitor's daughter from a suburb of Sydney.

Then there is the other side of Janus Weathercock's exile, supported by evidence rather than wild supposition and faux-outrage. It comes from the written testimonials of those who knew Wainewright in Van Diemen's Land.

Dr Bedford had testified in October 1840 in support of Wainewright's petition for a free pardon that he had known him since he had arrived in the colony and that he had always conducted himself with great propriety.

Then there was his application for a ticket-of-leave in 1844, attended with no fewer than five testimonials from the hospital staff.

James Fitzgerald, of the hospital purveyor's department, wrote that he had known him for six years and had never heard any complaint against him. "He has been under my immediate supervision for the greater part of the time and I have always noticed the steady and respectful manner in which he has behaved himself, by which…..he has acquired the good will and respect of the officers of the Medical Department."

The house surgeon wrote: "In addition to an unvarying propriety of demeanour, he has rendered me on many occasions important service of such early information of malpractices in progress or in contemplation as enabled me to interfere with advantage in the position in which I am placed". It seems he might have been informing on other patients.

One of the testimonials from Dr Mair was written in June 1843 at Dr Clarke's request. "He has been in this hospital as a patient since 12th January 1842, laboring (sic) under a diversity of symptoms all indicating an enfeebled state of the system generally, and a peculiar proneness to gastric and nervous irritation.

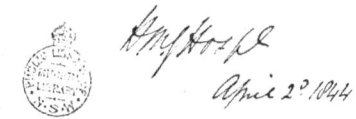

A raft of testimonials accompanied Wainewright's applications for an easing of his sentence and confound his reputation as a monster. This one from a house surgeon speaks of his 'unvarying propriety of demeanour' but also suggests he was a bit of a tell-tale, reporting on others misdemeanours.

*Mitchell Library, Sydney*

"This bodily weakness is such as effectually to prevent his being employed by the Government in any kind of laborious occupation, but I am of the opinion that he might have his talents as an artist turned to good account if he were permitted to exercise them free from the restraint necessarily imposed upon him...

"..........I consider him a man of superior attainments and I should feel happy if an indulgence could be granted him".

Clarke himself, who put forward the application paid tribute to this good conduct. A ticket-of-leave would improve his health and allow him to "use his superior talents as an artist to provide for his own wants and cease to be a burthen (sic) to the Government".

He had never been charged with misconduct in the colony, said a secretary's note attached to the petition.

It was, as we know, refused, but the significance of the testimonials is that they cover the whole 10 years he was in Van Diemen's Land, and show exemplary behaviour, though there is no mention of his opium-chewing, not only because it was probably thought unremarkable, but also because it may well have been given to him to alleviate the symptoms of whatever disease he was suffering from, described in one book, without any evidence, as disseminated sclerosis.

A "steady and respectful manner" engendering "goodwill and respect", "a man of superior attainments" with "an unvarying propriety of demeanour" - this convict was far removed from the monster that the self-righteous Victorians wanted to label him. Much closer in fact to Lamb's "kind and light-hearted Janus" and another friend's tribute to a "facetious, good-hearted fellow". He was an enigma to the end.

# CHAPTER 24

# THE RECKONING

Who killed Helen Abercromby? There is little doubt. It was Eliza her half-sister. In the civil insurance trials of 1835, the family's servant Harriet Grattan had testified under oath that on the afternoon of Helen's death, Eliza administered a powder in jelly that had not been prescribed by Dr Locock. That, declared the Attorney-general, had been the "fatal cup".

The establishment of guilt in a murder case depends, among other causes, on two standard issues - motive and opportunity. There was, of course, no murder case brought, but Eliza met the two tests. The motive was clear; she had conspired to defraud the insurance companies from the start by dragging Helen around London insuring her for huge sums of money, a large part of which would come to her husband on Helen's death. The opportunity was also obvious. An enfeebled Helen, prostrate with sickness on her bed in Conduit Street, was in no position to refuse any medicine that was offered to her, especially as the bitter strychnine's taste was hidden by sweetness of a jelly.

The judge at the trial had called Helen's death "pregnant with suspicion"; the Attorney-general had pointed his finger metaphorically at Eliza and named her as the perpetrator who had administered that 'fatal cup'. It is true that he subsequently said there was no imputation involved, but that was because the judge had ruled against the way he was putting forward his case: not only was it likely to prejudice the minds of the jury, the judge had said, but it was irrelevant anyway as to whether the policy was valid or not.

Today, after a suspicious death such as Helen's, there would have to be an inquest and charges of manslaughter or murder brought. But in 1830 there was no forensic evidence available, medical men had testified to the best of their knowledge that there were no suspicious causes of death and lives in the 19th century were often all too brief.

One of the most remarkable things about the Wainewright case is the way that Eliza's family life carried on without him after Helen's death, as if her part in it had never happened.

Everything proceeded as normal after this traumatic event. Madalina, mourning her sister, went to live with Eliza and Griffiths, chose Eliza as a witness at her wedding to Benjamin Wheatley and later let their solicitor help the poverty-stricken Eliza in her attempts to gain access to her settlement. Son Griffiths, too, was to stay with his mother for many years.

Did they all still believe that it was "oysters and wet feet" that had killed Helen? Were they not suspicious about Helen's life being insured for huge sums just before her death?

The burden of guilt subsequently fell entirely upon Wainewright, who has been blamed and excoriated ever since. In criminal law, under the principle of joint enterprise, a person can be found guilty for another's crime. It is a very old law, originally enacted to deter people from being seconds to duellists.

Under joint enterprise, Wainewright was undoubtedly guilty. He was an accessory before the fact. He had conspired in the insurance frauds and made Helen sign over an insurance policy to benefit him as she lay dying. He had been complicit in the creation of her two wills.

But he did not give the fatal dose, though his offer to Henry Smith to tell all about the case to the Home Secretary to save himself from transportation, shows he knew "where the Medicines were procured".

More significantly it adds: "You may inform the Secretary of State that I am ready to make such depositions as will put Mrs W's affair already very strange in a new light."

An inference that can be drawn from this is that he was going to say that he was not the prime mover in the case - it was Eliza. We know that in the years up to the murder Wainewright was a feckless fop, recklessly borrowing and squandering money. Of Eliza's character nothing is known other than Barry Cornwall's description of her as a "sharp-eyed, self-possessed woman, dressing in showy, flimsy finery" who obeyed Wainewright's humours and assisted his needs, but then Cornwall had no good to say of anyone involved in this affair.

It could be argued that she was just obeying Wainewright's instructions, but he was catastrophically disorganised and her involvement in the insurance frauds and the killing of Helen was so complete that she must have been the main perpetrator.

Consider the fact that Helen made 15 visits to different insurance offices between March and October 1830. But it was not Wainewright who was her constant companion - it was Eliza, who was with her on 12 occasions, putting forward unlikely reasons for effecting the policies. Wainewright was present on only a couple of the visits.

Was it then Eliza, six years after the forgeries, to which she had consented, aided and even been the prime mover according to her husband, and driven to desperation by his irresponsibility, his recourse to the money-lenders and the family's looming destitution, who had hatched the whole plot to cash in on the insurance policies? She was the Lady Macbeth in the drama, driven by resolution and cunning.

At the Hope Insurance Office, it was Eliza who dictated a form of assignment transferring the benefit of Helen's £2,000 policy to Wainewright. She did the same at the Palladium. Two of the documents that Sharpus the moneylender had, purportedly written by Wainewright, were in his wife's handwriting, according to his solicitor.

Was she the brains behind the entire enterprise and was the pressure so severe that she was prepared to sacrifice her half-sister, 13 years' younger, to extricate them from their plight?

The answer must be yes. She became the archetypal female poisoner, administering the fatal dose of strychnine to her weakened half-sister then waiting to claim the rewards that would transform their lives.

But then we come to the issue of the other two deaths for which Wainewright was blamed, that of his uncle George and his mother-in-law Mrs Abercromby. Both died sudden deaths that benefited him and Eliza. The only evidence of poisoning in their deaths was Harriet Grattan's statement that they had died in similar ways to Helen. But that is not proof of murder, there was no sighting of a 'fatal cup' being administered and people die in agony for many different reasons.

However, Uncle George died very soon after the Wainewrights arrived at Linden House, which they then inherited. Mrs Abercromby died with a week of making a will which benefitted her daughter. Again, events were "pregnant with suspicion".

Eliza might well have despatched Uncle George to gain possession of the desirable country house in Turnham Green, but would she really have killed her own mother for the small bequest she received? It cannot be ruled out as it might have been part of the plan to get her out of the way so that the grand stratagem of Helen's insurance policies could be put into action which would create far greater riches.

Perhaps her poisoning was the last desperate resort; there may have been a plan to send her abroad, then claim she had disappeared and was probably dead. But by the autumn of 1830 all the funds had disappeared on buying insurance policies and there was none left to pay for such a dubious enterprise.

As for Wainewright, blamed for all three deaths by everyone since, his compulsive behaviour in acquiring huge numbers of artistic objects, squandering vast sums of money, swindling the Bank of England when he knew he could be hanged for it and falling into the hands of moneylenders, displays a total lack of responsibility, possibly caused by his severe mental illness after leaving the army.

Did he suffer from what was called in the 1830s a 'moral insanity' which made him a psychopathic killer? He seems too feckless, disorganised and weak-minded to put all these careful homicides into place, whereas Eliza was meticulous in planning all the visits to the insurance offices and solicitors to construct the insurance fraud.

The verdict on the deaths of Uncle George and Mrs Abercromby has to be the Scots 'not proven', even though the circumstantial evidence is strong. But of Eliza's guilt in Helen's death, there is no doubt.

Thompson, the Eagle's dogsbody in the pursuit of Wainewright, was said to have told his boss Henry Smith that Wainewright had used morphine and strychnine. But Smith relayed this tale many years later to the novelist Bulwer Lytton, who he was trying to impress with his part in the affair. Not only is it hearsay, there is no indication that morphine was used..

"Wainewright the Poisoner" as he has been known ever since, rather than being the deadly monster he has been painted was, in fact, the hapless creature of his controlling wife Eliza. He was complicit in her nefarious schemes, he knew Helen was to die, but it was Eliza that killed her.

In Van Diemen's Land, rather than being the fiend with his arm buried up to the elbow in someone's guts, he was a model prisoner for 10 years, attested to by the medical staff who knew him so well.

Helen's death, rather than producing huge sums of money, sundered the family. Eliza went on to live in dire poverty and near-starvation for years, burdened with a son who was farmed out as a child, then, as an adult, often out of work. Wainewright spent years in exile in France in penury, then another 10 years in what to him was a living hell on the other side of the world. Both were wracked by sickness and hopelessness.

The dandy and his wife both paid a very heavy price for their lavish lifestyle. But they were never charged or convicted of the crime that did for poor Helen and possibly two other of their relations.

## CHAPTER 25

## "MY NICE PROMISING BOY"

With Wainewright dead, what of the murderer Eliza and of Griffiths "my nice, promising boy"? He turned out to be very promising indeed, as I have discovered. Previous authors have suggested that in 1851 he moved to America with his mother, then returned to England, discovering the family talent for painting under the wing of a wealthy woman. This is pure speculation.

What we do know is that he was married in London on May 16th 1857 at St James', Sussex Gardens, Paddington. His bride was Mary Jane Maitland, a widow some three years older than himself and the daughter of a Hertfordshire clergyman, the Rev. William Wollaston Pym.

Griffiths, who was by then 29, gives both his own and his father's occupation as 'esquire' on the marriage certificate. The pretence that Wainewright père was still of the gentry was being kept up almost a decade after his death in disgrace, and there is no indication of how Griffiths was keeping up appearances.

It is surprising that his mother Eliza was not a witness as she had been at Madalina's wedding. The marriage certificate was signed by Henrietta Pym and William Acheson, one of Wainewright's solicitors.

By the following year Griffiths' life had changed dramatically, as had Eliza's. I have discovered that he, Mary Jane and his mother moved to Canada, probably at the behest of Acheson, who had mercantile interests there. The couple's first child, Claude Beauchamp Wainewright, was born in October 1858 in Brighton, Ontario, a town on the north shore of Lake Ontario between Toronto and Trenton.

The 1861 census shows Griffiths' occupation as 'clerk' and that Eliza, then 65, was living with them, as was six-year-old Lionel Maitland, born in Australia. Was he Mary Jane's son by her previous husband? Beatrice followed two years later, Edward a year on, and then Constance. The family was obviously doing well; there were two Irish maids named as B and M Lilley living with them.

But Eliza moved back to England shortly afterwards, we do not know why, and she died on February 12th, 1863 at the age of 67.

She had been living in what was then the hamlet of Clay Hill, which lay between Bushey and Bushey Heath in Hertfordshire, sharing a house called Hill Side with Mary Lydia Richardson, who was with her there when she died. The death certificate records that she had been suffering from pneumonia for 10 days. She had outlived her husband for more than 15 years.

The two women had not been there for long. The census returns for two years earlier show that living at Hill Side in 1861 were a retired dairyman, George Garratt, his wife (also named Eliza) and a 14-year-old servant girl. Curiously, Eliza Wainewright's daughter-in-law, Mary Jane, was also to die in a house called Hill Side, but thousands of miles away.

The end of Eliza, the real poisoner, from pneumonia in 1863 not long after her return from Canada. She had outlived her husband by 15 years and not seen him for nearly 30.

In the death certificate under 'occupation' it states: "Widow of Wainewright. Christian name not known." There is no record of any will and there is no likeness of her existing; Wainewright was not known to have drawn or painted one. All that exists of her is a few well-written letters asking for charity.

Eliza remains an enigma who bore a heavy responsibility for what she had done more than 30 years previously when she killed her half-sister. Whether she also bore a burden of guilt, we do not know; there is no record of any expression of remorse or regret. Griffiths, at least, seems not to have judged her, as they remained together almost to her end.

At Trenton, close to where Griffiths was living, there is still a large military base and it seems that it was here that he became a lieutenant in the militia, a reserve army helping British troops to defend the Dominion of Canada against threats from Frenchmen and Fenians. He was in the 7th Battalion Fusiliers, according to the Militia List.

New research in Canada for this book has shown that in 1866 he was part of the force which put down a Fenian incursion – an attempt by Irish republicans in America to invade Canada. By 1870, he was a major in command of a company of the Ontario Battalion of Rifles sent to what is now Manitoba to quash the Red River Rebellion – an attempt at self-determination by the *mètis* – people of mixed European and Indian blood. Ironically, both rebellions served only to reinforce the Canadian move towards confederation.

The 1871 census sees Griffiths, occupation *Gentleman,* living in the lakeshore town of Colborne, a few miles from his first home in Brighton, with his wife, twelve-year-old Claude, Beatrice, Edward and Constance. Lionel, the mystery child, has disappeared. The family now have one live-in Irish maid, Alice.

Griffiths retired with the rank of honorary lieutenant–colonel – well above his substantive rank - but returned to the Fusiliers under a Militia General Order No 4 of 4 Oct 1878:

*To be Adjutant, with rank of Captain: Griffiths Wainewright, from Retired List of Lieutenant-Colonels, vice Gorman, promoted Major.*

He finally retired in June 1881 and resumed his title, which he was to use for the rest of his life.

He had moved from Ontario to Calgary, in Alberta, where his two daughters married and settled down, and then around 1900, he and Mary Jane moved to Vancouver, the booming city on the west coast where his son Claude had just become the manager of the British Columbia Printing and Engraving Co.

In December 1902 Mary Jane died of heart disease at the age of 79. They had been married for more than 45 years. Her death was reported in Vancouver's *Province* newspaper on Friday, December 3rd:

> *Death of Mrs. Wainewright*
> *After a brief illness, Mrs. Wainewright, wife of LieutenantColonel Wainewright, and oldest daughter of the late Rev. William Wollaston Pym, Herts, and sister of William. The deceased lady has resided here about two years, having previously lived in Calgary. She leaves a son and two daughters, Mr Claude Wainewright of this city, and Mrs. Richards and Mrs. Stone of Calgary. The funeral will take place from Mr. Claude Wainewright's residence, 1242 Eighth Avenue, Fairview, at 2 o'clock on Saturday.*

Of Edward, there is no mention, suggesting he predeceased his mother.

Griffiths lived alone in Vancouver in some style until he was over 80, but when he became unable to care for himself in 1909, he moved in with his son Claude and wife Margaret, at their home in Fairview. He died there on August 16th, 1914, at the age of 86 after a three-month illness. The death certificate, signed by a Dr Ford, gives "senile decay" as the cause.

It was now his turn to appear in *The Daily Province* as the paper had become known:

> *Wainewright on August 16 at the residence of his son, C B Wainewright, 1242 Eighth avenue west, Lieut.col. Griffiths Wainewright, aged 86. The funeral will take place from the above address on Tuesday, 18th at 10 a.m.*

He is buried in Mount View cemetery, Vancouver.

The details given by Claude to the Registrar put the father's name as 'Thomas Wainewright', occupation 'Militia-man'; the Griffiths is not included. And there is a mystery about his mother's name. It is not given as Eliza Frances Wainewright, as she had appeared in the Canadian census, but as Fanny Cooper-Ward, suggesting she was then known as Fanny rather than Eliza; the *Ward,* of course, was her maiden name, the *Cooper,* her father's Christian name, which is not on her birth certificate, but was used by her siblings. It seems unlikely that it was a conscious effort on behalf of the grandson to distance her from the family surname and was probably just a result of confusion, after all, by that time she had been dead for more than 50 years.

Claude prospered in the printing business and even produced a pamphlet of his own on *The Wainewright expansion centre-board: for yachts, sail boats, skiffs, canoes, etc.* in 1925 and in 1939 he took out a patent for a 'sock stretcher and dryer'. He lived even longer than his father, dying

> Griffiths not only made a success of his life after a deeply unpromising start, but lived to a ripe old age. On his death certificate, Eliza's name is given as Fanny Cooper-Ward, reverting for some reason to her second Christian name and her own family's surname.
>
> *British Columbia Division of Vital Statistics*

in 1951 at the age of 92, another event recorded in the *Daily Province*.

> *Wainewright Passed away July 12, 1951, Claude Beauchamp Wainewright, 3166 W. 11 th Ave. in his 93rd year. Survived by 1 son, Victor Charles, Vancouver; 1 daughter, Miss Winnifred (sic) at home; 2 grandchildren. Funeral service Saturday at 1 p. m. in Simmons*

& McBride Funeral Chapel, Broadway at Maple St, Rev. Conway Jones officiating.

The Wainewright name was carried on by his surviving son, Victor Charles, a clerk in the Imperial Bank of Canada. Claude's daughter Winnifred never married and lived with her father until his death.

But there had been at least two other sons - Lionel was an accountant at the British Columbia Trust Corporation and there was a third son named after Mary Jane's father - Wollaston Guy Wainewright, a clerk with the Canadian Pacific Railway. The three boys were still living with their father in 1914, according to street directories of the period, but as the obituary notes, only Victor was still alive in 1951 – and he had only three years to live.

Claude had two grandchildren, though his obituary does not specify the sex. Today, there are several Wainewrights in the telephone directories of Ontario, and many without the 'e' in Vancouver, though none is called either Thomas or Griffiths. There has been a temptation to ring them, just to see if they could trace their lineage to the distinguished lieutenant-colonel, and then to tell them of the infamy in which their name was held more than 150 years ago.

But kinder thoughts have prevailed.

# APPENDIX 1

## *APPEAL TO HOME SECRETARY 1837*

To the Right Honourable Lord John Russell, Her Majesty's Principal Secretary of State for the Home Department.

The Humble Petition of Thomas Griffiths Wainewright Most Humbly Sheweth

That your Petitioner was at the Session holden for the Jurisdiction of the Central Criminal Court at Justice Hall in the Old Bailey on the 3rd day of July last indicted upon two several charges of feloniously knowingly and fraudulently demanding and endeavouring to have transferred assigned, sold and conveyed the sums of £2250 and £3000 new 4 per cent Annuities the property of Robert Wainewright, Edward Smith Foss and Edward Foss transferred by virtue of forged letters of Attorney, to which indictments Your Petitioner by the advice of his Professional adviser and his own inclination Pleaded Guilty. There being two other indictments against him for forging the said Instruments, upon which no Evidence was offered on behalf of the Crown. Your Petitioner was acquitted and Your Petitioner was thereupon sentenced to be Transported for his natural life.

That although your Petitioner pleaded Guilty he was still desirous that the whole circumstances of the Transactions should be known to the Court in hopes that the Judgment to be passed upon him might possibly be affected thereby and for this purpose when called up to receive sentence Your Petitioner applied to the presiding judge the Recorder of the City of London, who referred Your Petitioner to Your Lordship saying he had no power to alter or mitigate the sentence to be passed on Your Petitioner.

That at an early age Your Petitioner formed a very injudicious marriage without the knowledge of any of his Relations which soon led him into difficulties and Embarrassments, but to guard against further involving himself Your Petitioner was induced to settle the said sum of £5000 upon his Wife for the benefit of any Children they might have, and in case of failure of Issue then in trust for Your Petitioner which sum was accordingly laid out in the Public Funds in the names of the said Robert Wainewright, Edward Smith Foss and Edward Foss as Trustees who for several Years paid the Dividends as they became due to Your Petitioner and at length in order to save trouble the Trustees gave Your Petitioner a power of Attorney to enable him to receive the Dividends himself which he continued to do for some time and at length in the Year 1823 his Wife then having no Children although several years married and Your Petitioner considering that he would eventually by the Terms of the settlement become entitled to the money and being embarrassed committed the crime which has placed Your Petitioner in his present degraded and most unhappy situation.

That although your Petitioner seeks not to excuse the crime, he yet ventures to suggest as a palliation that the Money obtained was originally his own and placed in the hands of Trustees for a specific object which had not then occurred nor was there any probability of such occurrence.

Your Petitioner therefore humbly Prays that Your Lordship will take all the circumstances of his unhappy Case into Your humane consideration and if in Your Lordship's Judgment they do not warrant any mitigation in point of time that Your Lordship will be pleased to interfere to soften the rigour of his sentence as far as may be consistent with humanity and Justice.

T.G. Wainewright.

*National Archives HO17/101*

## APPENDIX 2

### 1840 PETITION FOR FREE PARDON. MARKED 2ND APPLICATION

Summary on cover:
The prisoner states that were many extenuating circumstances ....that his sufferings have been great & that he has behaved in the Colony. He prays for Pardon in order that he may return to France and devote himself to literary pursuits.
Presented by T Von Holst
19, Nassau St, Middlesex Hospital

To The Right Honourable Lord Normanby
Principal Secretary of State
The humble Petition of Thomas Griffiths Wainewright
Respectfully Sheweth

That your Lordship's Petitioner was tried at the Old Bailey on the third day of July 1837 and received sentence of Transportation for life. That Petitioner arrived in this Colony on the Ship Susan in November 1837, and was forthwith placed in the Public Works.
That Petitioner from the Public Works, was transferred to the Service of Edward S.P. Bedford Esq. of the Colonial Medical Department, in whose employ he still remains.
That the conduct of your Lordship's Petitioner during his sojourn in his Colony has been such as to obtain the approbation of those under whose control he has been immediately stationed, and the more especially of his actual Master aforesaid, by whose council (sic) Petitioner now ventures to submit his case with some

attenuating details for the purpose of inducing your Lordship to permit him to return to that Country *La France* where previously to his transportation he had resided seven years, and where alone his abilities such as they are, can be rendered available.

Moreover in England, though pardoned, he would be ever excluded from the Society of Gentlemen, Whereas in the other land his case, though stated without alleviation by the English Consul Hamilton, excited only the commiseration of those respectable Frenchmen who became cognisant thereof and procured him the good offices of one well known as an antiquarian, poet, composer and Litterateur viz Pierre Hedouin, Batonnier of the *avocats* of the Boulognaise, who furnished him with most flattering recommendation to friends at Paris as *savant Anglais* also deeply versed in Music, les Beaux Arts and the Literature and Philosophy of Germany, France and England and here, as a Man's associates have ever been held to illustrate his turn and *moeurs* Petitioner submits a few names of his former intimates Dr Gooch, B. West P.R.A. Richard Westall R.A., Hugo Foscolo, Dante Cary, Charles Lamb

(Elia), Sir Thomas Lawrence, H. Fuseli, P.P. Constable R.A., Alfred Chalon R.A., Thos Hood, Francis Douce, F.R.S, The ill-fated John Scott of the Champion and "Paris", Allan Cunningham, Thomas Stothard, Dr Symmons the Defender of Milton, Dr G. Pearson, Thomas Phillips Esq. R.A., William G. Ottley F.R.S., William Daniel R.A., Barry Cornwall (B.W. Procter) and Sir Edward Brace K.C.B.

Your Lordship's Petitioner was charged with a forgery committed thirteen years prior to his capture, and with regard to that crime he avers that the fund which created the Stock he is charged with transferring by such forgery was originally his own, derived from his Father, and settled by himself in the names of Trustees, giving himself a life interest; His Wife,

After his decease to inherit in failure of issue, in which case she could only claim the annual interest. The Principal to devolve on the issue of his and her body.

These contingencies failing the stock was to revert to Petitioner and that at that time (now upwards of sixteen years since) Petitioner neither had or was likely to have children, having been married nearly six years. That the crime was committed, his Wife consenting and aiding, as the forged Power manifests. That encouraged by the opinions generally expressed in France and England as to the venial character of this individual offence, as compared with the usual cases of Forgery (crimes against society) he resolved to trust to the leniency of this prosecutor often in other cases heretofore displayed, hoping that the animus or intent to plunder no-one but himself, and many years having elapsed since the commission thereof, might induce the award of a short imprisonment. Moreover moved thereto by special advice of the Governor of Newgate, Mr Cope, at the last minute, he revoked his plea of not Guilty and offered no defence. But he has been cruelly disappointed and finds himself classed with, and more heavily punished, than Men whose whole lives have been one chain of crimes.

And he prays your Lordship to consider whether the agonising separation from all which makes life worth holding to a thinking being, and the compelled association with men whose language and sentiments startle the oldest London thieves, and has in fact shaken Petitioner's reason, has not already made as much atonement as a more obtuse and indurated criminal may have completed in twenty years. His corporal pangs he lets pass, though two years at the barrow have made sore inroads in a frame always sickly, as Dr Locock of Hanover Square can testify.

His Excellency the Governor authorises this your Petitioner's Suit, in granting which your Lordship will not return a thief to his former tortuous ways, but a true Pilgrim (with Schiller, Novalis and Coleridge) in search of the Ideal, who will diligently from time to time give with Letters and painted forms such indication of his progress in that gorgeous region as may justify your discrimination, your sympathy and your mercy. Your Petitioner has been many years acquiring the materials for an extensive Psychological work on the Analogies of the Imagination properly illustrated by the brain products of Dante, Pindar, Goethe, Phidias, Palladio, Gluck, Beethoven, Giotto, Michael Agnolo (sic). Sansovino, Eschylus, Polycletus, Orcagna, Lessing, Calderona, Pergolese, Corneille, etc etc. and also on canvas to vivify afresh the effete limbs of classic art, for a combat against the debasing coarseness of the Dutch School and the fantasies of the Beauty Book style, having been heartened thereunto by his late friends Lawrence, Fuseli and Westall. Mr Phillips the distinguished Painter can speak to the truth of this assertion, and to his powers some ten years back they are now by thought and study, doubled. Have pity on a mind now nearly strangled, but worthy perhaps of life, and remember that thereon your word has the potency of a God. Life or Death hangs on your Lordship's decision

That your Lordship's Petitioner relying with confidence on his general good conduct and the veracity of the above statement coupled with the annexed Testimonial Humbly hopes that your Lordship will be pleased to grant him a Free Parson.

And your Lordship's Petitioner will as in duty bound, ever pray etc. etc ...

*National Archives HO17/101*

## APPENDIX 3

## PETITION FOR TICKET OF LEAVE 18 APRIL 1844

"To His Excellency Sir John Eardly-Wilmot, Bart., Lieut. – Governor of Van Diemen's Land etc. etc.

The Humble Petition of T. Griffiths Wainewright praying the Indulgence of a Ticket of Leave.

To palliate the boldness of this application he offers the statement ensuing.
That *seven* years past he was arrested on a charge of Forging and acting, on a power of attorney to sell stock *13 years previous*. Of which (tho' looking for little credence) he avers his entire innocence. He admits knowledge of the actual Committer, gained tho' some years after the fact. Such however were their relative positions that to have disclosed it would have made him infamous where any human feeling is manifest. Nevertheless, by his Counsel's direction, he entered the plea not *guilty*, to allow him to adduce the *'circonstance attenuante'* (extenuating circumstances) viz.: That the money (£5,200) appropriated was, without quibble, *his own*, derived from his parents.
An hour before his appearing to plead he was trepanned (thro' the just, but deluded Govr of Newgate) into withdrawing his plea, by a promise, in such case, of a *punishment* merely nominal. The Same *purporting* to issue from y$^e$ *Bank Parlour*, but in fact, from the Agents of certain *Insurance Companies* interested to a heavy amount (£16,000) in compassing his legal *non*-existence. He pleaded 'Guilty' and was forthwith hurried, stunned

with such ruthless perfidy, to the Hulks at Portsmouth, and thence, in 5 days, aboard the 'Susan,' sentenced to a life in a land (to him) a moral sepulchre.

As a ground for your mercy he submits with great diffidence his foregone condition of a Life during 43 years of freedom.

A *Descent*, deduced, thro' Family Tradition & Edmonstone's Heraldry, from a Stock not the least honoured in Cambria. Nurtured with all appliances of ease and comfort. School'd by his relative the well-known Philologer and Bibliomaniac Chas. Burney D.D. brother to Mdme D'Arblay and the companion of Cooke. Lastly such a modest competence as afforded the *mental* necessaries of Literature, Archæology, Music and the Plastic Arts; while his pen and brush introduced him to the notice and friendship of Men whose fame is European. The Catalogues of Somerset House Exhibns, the Literary Pocket Book, indicate his earlier pursuits, and the Ms., left behind in Paris, attest at least his industry.

Their titles imply the objects to which he has, *to this date*, directed all his energies. 'A Philosophical Theory of Design, as concerned with the *Loftier* Emotions, shewing its deep action on Society, drawn from the Phidean-Greek and early Florentine Schools,' (the result of 17 years' study) illustrated with numerous plates executed with conscientious accuracy, in one vol. Atlas folio. 'An Æsthetic and Psychological Treatise on the *Beautiful*, or the Analogies of Imagination and Fancy, as existed in *Poesy, Verse, Painting, Sculpture, Music* or *Architecture*,' to form four Vols folio; with a profusion of Engravings by the best Artists of Paris, Munich, Berlin, Dresden and Wien. 'An Art Novel' in 3 vols. and a collection of Fantasie, Critical Sketches &c. selected partly from *Blackwood*, the *Foreign Review* & the *London Mag.*

All these were nearly ready for, *one* actually at press. Deign, Your Excellency! to figure to yourself my actual condition during 7 years; without *friends, good-name* (the breath of life) or *Art*— (the fuel to it with *me*). Tormented at once by Memory & Ideas struggling for outward form & realization, barred up from increase of knowledge, & deprived of the exercise of profitable or even *decorous* speech.

Take pity Your Excellency! and grant me the power to shelter my eyes from Vice in her most revolting and sordid phase, and my ears from a jargon of filth & blasphemy that would outrage the cynism (*sic*) of Parny himself. Perhaps this clinging to the lees of a vapid life may seem as *base, unmanly*, arguing rather a plebeian than a liberal & gentle descent, but your Excellency! the wretched *Exile* has a child! and *Vanity*, (sprung from the praise of Flaxman, *Coleridge, Charles Lamb,* Stothard, Rd. Westall, *De la Roche, Cornelius, Lawrence* and the God of his worship, *Fuseli*) whispers that the *follower of the Ideal* might even yet achieve another reputation than that of a *Faussaire*. Seven years of steady demeanour may in some degree promise that no indulgence shall ever be abused by Your Excellency's miserable Petitioner      T. G. WAINEWRIGHT."

## SUMMARY PRODUCED FOR THE GOVERNOR-GENERAL

Thomas Griffiths Wainewright per 'Susan' petitions for some Indulgence, declaring his innocence of the offence for which he is now suffering - he has been six years and a half in the colony under a Life Sentence and produces very good testimonials - he has been for nearly two years and a half a patient in the Colonial Hospital and Dr Clarke expresses an opinion that it would ameliorate his bodily ailments if his mind could be relieved by the extension to him of some Indulgence - he has never been charged with misconduct in the Colony.

*16th May 1844*

*Mitchell Library, Sydney. AW15/1*

## SELECT BIBLIOGRAPHY

Acres, W Marston
*Bank of England from Within*
Oxford, 1931

Balmanno, Mary
*Pen and Pencil*
Appleton & Co, 1858

Bateson, Charles
*The Convict Ships 1787-1868*
Brown, Son & Ferguson, 1959

Branch-Johnson. W
*The English Prison Hulks*
C. Johnson, 1957

Buckingham, John
*Bitter Nemesis: The Intimate History of Strychnine*
CRC, Boca Raton, 2007

Burney, Ian.
*Poison, Detection and the Victorian Imagination.*
Manchester UP, 2006

Cannon, Richard
*Historical Record of the 16th*
Parker Furnival &. Park,1848

Collins, P.
*Dickens and Crime*
Macmillan, 1962

Crosland, Newton Mrs
*Landmarks of a Literary Life*
Sampson Low Marston, 1893

Crossland, Robert
*Wainewright in Tasmania*
OUP Melbourne 1956

Curling, Jonathan
*Janus Weathercock*
Nelson, 1938

Ellis, Havelock
*The Criminal*
Walter Scott, 1901

Faulkner, Thomas
*Antiquities of Brentford Chiswick
& Ealing*
Simkin Marshall,1845

Finlayson, Robert
*An essay to the Captains of the Royal Navy....on preserving the health of crews*
The Pamphleteer, 1825

Forster, John
*Life of Charles Dickens*
Dent, 1969

Griffiths, Arthur
*Chronicles of Newgate*
Chapman and Hall, 1884

Hazlitt Carew, W (ed)
*Essays & Criticisms of Thomas Griffiths Wainewright*
Reeves & Turner, 1880

Leeson, R (ed)
*Hayek: A Collaborative Biography Part III, Fraud, Fascism and Free Market Religion.*
Palgrave Macmillan, 2014

Lewis. Samuel
*A Topographical Dictionary of Ireland*
Lewis, 1837

Lytton, Earl of
*Life of Edward Bulwer*
Macmillan, 1913

Lytton, Earl of
*Lucretia*
Routledge, 1853

Masson, David
*de Quincy*
Macmillan, 1888

McCormick, Donald
*The Red Barn Mystery*
John Long, 1967

Proctor, B W (Barry Cornwall)
*Autobiographical Fragment*
Geo. Bell, 1877

Raymond, John (ed)
*Reminiscences and Recollections of Capt Gronow*
Bodley Head 1964

Rimmer, W G
*Portrait of a hospital*
Hobart Hospital, 1981

Robson, L L.
*Convict settlers of Australia*
Melbourne UP, 1994

Seccombe, Thomas (ed)
*Twelve Bad Men*
Fisher Unwin, 1929

Shaw, A.G. L.
*Convicts and the Colonies*
Faber, 1966

Stone, C R and Tyson P
*Old Hobart Town and environs 1802-1855*
Pioneer, 1978

Thornbury, Walter
*Old Stories Retold*
Chapman & Hall, 1870

Thorwald, Jurgen
*Proof of Poison*
Thames and Hudson, 1966

Young & Handcock (ed)
*English Historical Documents 1833-1874*
Eyre & Spottiswoode, 1956

Vaulbert de Chantilly, Marc
(in) *Under the Hammer*
Oak Knoll Press/British Library 2001

*Wainewright the Poisoner*
*An example of Andrew Motion's 'high scholarship'*
Vanity Press, 2000

Whorton, J C.
*The Arsenic Century*
Oxford, 2010

Wilde, Oscar
*Pen, Pencil and Poison*
Fortnightly Review, 1889/1

# MAJOR SOURCES

## NATIONAL ARCHIVES, LONDON, UNLESS OTHERWISE SPECIFIED

| | |
|---|---|
| Middlesex Criminal Register | 1837 HO 26/43 |
| Convict Transportation Register | 1837-8 HO11/11 |
| Tasmania Pardons | 1847/8 HO 10/56-60 |
| Convict Hulks Attested List | 1837 HO 8/53 |
| Colonial Office, Tasmania Individuals' Correspondence T-Z | 1847 CO 280/2, 280/247 |
| Foreign Office Correspondence, France | 1835 FO 27/499-500 FO 146/158 FO 146/161 |
| Criminal Petitions | 1837 HO 1313 HO 17/101 |

Bank of England Letter Books    1835
G23/55

Newgate Calendar    1837
HO 77/44

Register of the York    1837-43
HO 8/15

Dispatches, Denison. Aug-Sept    1847
CO 280/211

Governors' Correspondence Index    1847-56
CO 714 150
IND 18616

Ships' Letters    ADM12/330

Captains' Logs    ADM/51

Indictments, Old Bailey    1837
CRIM 4/64

Record Book, Colonial Offences    CO 10/51
P242

Regimental Returns, 16th Foot    1815-16
WO 17/291
295
WO 17 275

Van Diemen's Land Convict
Discipline    1838
CO 283/80

Imperial Life Insurance
Court of Directors minutes
    1830-5
    12/60B
    Guildhall
    Library

Eagle Insurance minutes
    Eagle Star
    Archives,
    Cheltenham

Bulwer Lytton archive
    D/EKC1
    14/41/42/43
    Hertfordshire
    Record Office

Bishop's Transcripts, St Nicholas,
Chiswick
    Metropolitan
    Archives
    X100/179

Shipping at Portsmouth and
Spithead
    1826
    Natl Maritime
    Museum

Van Diemen's Land petitions
    Mitchell
    Library,
    Sydney

Record Book, Colonial Offences
    11/1837
    Vol 48. P 28
    Tasmania
    Archives

# ARMY DOCUMENTS

The Army List                1814-15

The Regimental Companion     1804

General Regulations and Orders  1815

## ACKNOWLEDGEMENTS

I have been fascinated by this story for many years and this book was begun a long time ago when the National Archives were still called the Public Record Office and based in a gloomy Victorian monstrosity in Chancery Lane where it took hours to obtain files. It has been completed with the ability to summon documents instantly with a click from all over the world. The book has proceeded in fits and starts over the years as other publications, books and proper journalistic work intervened. Having now had the time to finish it in has been a great pleasure.

I would like to thank, in no particular order, Deirdre Simmons in Vancouver for her research into the fate of Griffiths and Eliza; Isobel Syed, of the Eagle Star archives in Cheltenham; Erika Ingham at the National Portrait Gallery; Simon Brown at Newstead Abbey; Nicholas Donaldson at the Colnaghi archive; the Nuttall family for permission to photograph Wainewright portraits at their home in Surrey, my daughter Sian Williams and her husband Paul Woolwich for proof-reading, my brother David for photographic work and Dr Edward Burns for psychiatric advice (on Wainewright's condition, not mine). The index is by Linda Haylock.

Thanks, too, to staff at the British Museum, National Archives, the British Library, the Bank of England, the National Maritime Museum, the National Army Museum, the Mitchell Library,

Sydney, the National Portrait Gallery, Canberra, the State Library of Tasmania and the Hertfordshire County Record Office.

Apologies to anyone who has been omitted. Any errors of fact or interpretation are entirely my responsibility.

John Price Williams

Eastbourne. October, 2017.

## ABOUT THE AUTHOR

John Price Williams is a journalist who worked in Fleet Street on the *Daily Telegraph* and *Observer* then at BBC News in London as producer and editor. He is a Fellow of the Royal Geographical Society and has written several books on classic cars.

# INDEX

Note: Ship titles, written works and legal cases are given in *italics*, as are the page numbers of drawings, paintings and photographs. The initials TGW refer to Thomas Griffiths Wainewright.

Abercromby, Frances (TGW's mother-in-law) 5, 33–5, 58, 240–1
Abercromby, Helen Phoebe Frances (TGW's sister-in-law)
  date of birth 34
  death 6, 80–94, 97, 99–102, 129, 131–4, 157, 167, 173, 236–42
  forms of assignment 78–9, 83, 239
  life insurance 59, 62–75, 90–3, 132, 134–5, 137, 139–40, 161, 169, 188–90
  move to Linden House 58
  pension plea 60–1
  sitting for portrait 46
  TGW's drawing of *68*
  watching course of mother's illness 59
  will 77–80, 87, 92–3, 106, 129–31, 139–40, 174, 188, 238
Abercromby, John Bateman (Lieutenant) 34–6
Abercromby, Madalina Rosa Hibernia Burdett
  birth 34
  commemorating Helen 108
  death 141
  Helen's provision for 71–2, 78, 87, 92–3, 129, 131, 174
  as Helen's sister 34, 46
  helping Eliza 216, 237
  husband's death 140–1
  marriage 58, 108, 237
  mourning deaths of mother and sister 90
  move to Linden House 58
  suing of insurance companies 158, 161, 188–90
  TGW's debt to future husband 69, 93
  theatre visit 80
  watching course of mother's illness 59
Abinger, Lord 130, 135, 137, 139–40, 158, 171

Acheson, Robert Shank 54, 174
Acheson, William 243–4
Adams, John Bodkin 131
Allen, A G 105–6
Allen, Walter 230
Alliance insurance company 63, 70–1, 74, 137
*Amalie v. Holst* 143, 146–7
Arabin, Sergeant 160
Aram, Eugene 165
army career
  Griffiths Wainewright 246
  John Bateman Abercromby 34–5, 137
  Thomas Griffiths Wainewright 20–9
arsenic 94–7, 224
Aston, Arthur 115–18, 121–2
Atkinson, John 54, 83, 92, 129–30, 174
Attorney-general *see* Campbell, Sir John; Pollock, Sir Frederick
Auguste, Monsieur 142–8

Balmanno, Mary 46
Bank of England
  attitude towards forgery 162–3
  discovery of forgeries 109–12, 117, 122
  efforts to retrieve TGW from France 121–2
  Eliza's position with 215–20
  inflation calculator 10, 73, 75, 111
  investment of bequest 15
  offer of betrayal 142–7
  role in proving case against TGW 151
  satisfaction at TGW's sentence 165
  swindle on 5, 16, 36, 51–4, 62, 93, 110–12, 117–18, 122, 212, 240–1
  wrangle with Foss 212, 214–15
Barrow, John 186
Barrow, Peter 186
Baudelaire, Charles 39
Bedford, Edward 198–200, 232
Bedford, William 199
Benomam, F A 101

betrayal, offer of 142–8
Bird, James 78
Blake, William 4, 17, 39, 45
Blessington, Lady 18, 230
Bock, Thomas 199
Bonaparte, Napoleon 28
Brett, P. 22–3
Browne, Hablot Knight 156
Brummel, George Bryan ("Beau") 104, 157
Buckingham, John 96, 102
Bulwer Lytton, Edward 100, 149, 163, 165, 223–6, 241
Burney, Charles 17
Burns, Edward 31–2
Butler, Martha Sarah *207*
Byron, George Gordon, 6th Baron 18–20, *19*

calomel 82, 102
Campbell, Sir John (Attorney-general) 138–9
Capper, John Henry 172
Cardigan, James Thomas Brudenell, 7th Earl (Lord Cardigan) 26
Carlyle, Thomas 41, 210
Castree, Philip 172
Catteron, Mr 51, 151
Chesham, Sarah 224
Christison, Robert 97
Clare, John 4, 38, 41, 43
Clarke, Frederick John 202–5, *205*, 208, 232, 234
Cleland, John 10–11
Cochrane, John 65
Coleridge, Samuel Taylor 18, 21, 39, 82, 210
Colnaghi family 20, 40–1, 50, 149, 223
confessions
    alleged 100, 169, 226
    fictional 6–7
    offer of 170–4
    tricked into 198
*Confessions of an English Opium Eater* 41, 100–1
convict ships 167, 170, 178–87, 191–2

Cook, John Parsons 99–100
Cook, Mr 113, 158–9, 170
Cooper-Ward, Fanny 248–9
   see also Wainewright, Eliza Frances
Cope, Mr 160–1, 211
Corder, William 123–7
Cornwall, Barry 38, 41, 43, 57, 107, 147, 238
Cornwall, Henry 86–7, 139
Cotton, Mary Ann 95
court cases 81, 97, 108, 113–14, 129–40, 152, 160–6, 188–90, 236
Cream, Neil 99
Crooke, William 228
Cruickshank, George 44–5
Curling, Jonathan 31, 67, 211
Cutmear, Jane and Lucy 200, *201*, 202

dandyism 17–18, 20, 37–9, 157
d'Artois, Comte 147
de Chantilly, Marc Vaulbert 7, 42, 103
de la Pommerais, Couty 73–4
de Pauw, Madame 73–4
de Quincey, Thomas 41–2, 100–1, 229
de Rigny, Comte 117–18, 121
Denham, John Charles 70–1
Denison, Sir William 194
Denman, Lord 188–9
d'Erlanger, Lady 20
Dickens, Charles 6, 79, 114, 130, 154–7, 179, 230–1
d'Ordre, Baron 106, 143, 146
d'Ordre, Sophie 106
d'Orsay, Alfred Guillaume Gabriel (Count d'Orsay) 18, 20
Duke of Wellington 110, 118, 120
Dyas, Richard 35

Eagle insurance company 64–6, 72, 74, 83, 90–1, 100, 113–14, 158–9, 163, 165, 167, 169–70, 172, 174, 188–90, 216, 225–6, 241
Eardley-Wilmot, Sir John 204, 208

Ellis, Havelock 31
*Emma Eugenia* 183, 185
Erle, Mr 130–1, 134, 137–9, 188–9
Evans, Richard 165

Fandango, Hannah 123–6, 128
*Fanny Hill* 10–12
"fatal cup" 6, 133, 138, 236, 240
Fauntleroy, Henry 53–4
Fitzgerald, James 232
Follett, Sir William Webb 130
Foreign Office 109–10, 113, 116, 121–2
Forrester, Daniel 112–14, 116–17, 119–22, 142, 145–6, 148–50
Forrester, John 112–13, 150
Forster, John 6, 14–15, 156, 229–30
Foss, Edward Smith (TGW's 1st cousin, once removed) 15, 20, 36, 51, 66, 110–12, 150–1, 204
Foss, Edward (TGW's 2nd cousin) 15, 51, 66–7, 150–1, 211–17, 219–21
Foss, Fanny 204
Frampton, W H 216–19
France
    strychnine 96
    TGW's flight to 103–4
    TGW's time spent in 106–10, 114–22, 135, 142, 158–9, 242
*Frances Charlotte* 186
Franklin, Sir John 179, 191–2, 202
Freshfield, James William 142, 145, 151
Freshfields 53, 110, 114–16, 119–21, 212, 214–15, 219
Fuseli, Henry 4–5, 39–40, 45–6, 58, 148–9

Galloway, John 25–7
Garratt, George 244
*George III* 3, 182
Gilmour, Joanna 202
Glen, Thomas 90
Globe insurance company 70–1, 74
Goldsmith, Oliver 9–10
Goody, Henry 162

279

Goulborn, Henry 112
Graham, Thomas 63–4, 88–9
Gramont, Duc de 47
Grattan, Harriet 76, 84–5, 132, 146, 174, 236, 240
Griffiths, Arthur 162
Griffiths, Elizabeth (TGW's grandmother) 12–13, 16, 32
Griffiths, George Edward (TGW's uncle) 5, 8, 14, 16, 21, 55–7, 59, 240–1
Griffiths, Isabella (RG's first wife) 9–10
Griffiths, Ralph (TGW's grandfather) 9–16, 32, 36, 49, 51–3, 57–8, 111
Gronow, Rees Howell (Captain Gronow) 37
Grute, Nicholas 64–5

Hall, John 185
Hall, Samuel 115
Hamilton, A 47
Hamilton, Andrew 71
Hamilton, William 114–16, 120–2
Handcocks, Sarah 56, 59, 76, 132, 139, 146, 174
Hanks, Edward 85, 87–8, 137–8
Hayek, Friedrich 128
Hazlitt, William Carew 4, 17, 41–2, 47, 50, 54, 89, 100, 147
Heaven, Joseph 186
Hedouin, Pierre 106
Henderson, Mr 130
Hilditch, Edward 183–5, 187, 191
Hobart Town 183–5, 187, 193–200, 202, 204–11, 220–1, 228, 230–1
Hood, Thomas 38
Hooper, Henry 180–1
Hope insurance company 72, 74, 78, 87, 92, 135, 169, 239
Hotten, John Camden 157
*Hougoumont* 181
Hughes, Robert 204
Hullmandel, Charles 49
Huntingdon, Mr 108, 114

Imperial insurance company 71–2, 74, 91–2, 106, 129–40, 158, 165, 188–9, 250
*Indefatigable* 180
Ingall, Samuel 71–2
insurance frauds 62–75, 90–3, 236, 238–41
　*see also* court cases
Ireland 24–8, 34–5
*Islam* 24

Jacob, Edward 212
Janus Weathercock 41–2, 47, 49–50, 223, 231–2, 235

Kenny, Tom 231
Kirk, Thomas 79

Lamb, Charles 4, 41, 43, 54, 58, 235
Laurie, Sir Peter 150–2, 155
Lawrence, Thomas 4, 43, 45, 58
Le Blanc, Mr 113, 158–9
Ledbitter, Mr 115
Leech, John 98
*Leviathan* 175
Lewis, Samuel 26
Lidderdale, Dr 91
Linden House 8, *11*
　bailiff in 76
　description of 7–9
　ensuring continuity at 62
　friends dining in splendour at 37, 107
　furnishings and effects 57–8, 69, 84
　grounds of 16
　large size of 12
　library cataloguer 108
　origins of name 8
　seller of contents 140
　standing as security 92
　sudden deaths at 8, 56, 59–60, 80–94
　TGW's house as young child 15
　TGW's inheritance of 240

TGW's place of birth 7
TGW's return to 8, 54–5
Linnell, John 17
Locock, Charles 81–91, 94, 101–2, 131–4, 137, 236
*London Magazine* 37, 41–2, 51, 100
Lord, Edward 202
*Lucretia* 224–5
Lys, Thomas 77–8

Mackintosh, Mr 111
Macready, William Charles 58, 79, 156
Mair, Dr 200, 232
Maitland, Lionel 244, 246
Maitland, Mary Jane 243–7
Marsh, James 97
Marten, Maria 123, 126–7
Masson, David 38
Maule, Mr 162, 217
McCormick, Donald 123–4, 128
McMahon, Thomas 186
M'Donald, Mr 210
*Memoirs of a Woman of Pleasure* 10–12
mental illness 30–3, 75, 241
Miller, Mary 95
Molesworth, Sir William 180
*Monthly Returns* 25–7
*Monthly Review* 9, 16–17, 56–8
Moore, Mary 126
Morris, William 96
Morton, A. 49
Motion, Andrew 6–7
Murray, John 18

Neatby, Henry 179
*Neva* 182
Newgate Prison 53, 153–60, 166, 175, 230
Nichol, Mr 76, 81
Nichol, Mrs 132
Normanby, Lord 197–8

Nuttall, George 203
Nuttall, Robert Kennedy 202–4, *203*

Oliver, Mr 113, 158–9
oysters 79–80, 84, 88–9, 132, 138, 237

Palladium insurance company 63–5, 70, 74, 77, 79, 92, 135, 169, 239
Palmer, Caroline 124–5, 128
Palmer, William 99–100
Payne, Matthew 89
Peacock, Walter Anderson 188
Peel, Robert 112–13
Pelican insurance company 64, 69, 74, 105, 158, 165, 169, 188
Phillips, Thomas 18–20
Pinel, Phillipe 32
*Platina* 187
poison
   availability of 94–7
   characteristics of administrators of 32–3
   court cases 131–4, 137–8, 171
   detection of 97–100
   Eliza as administrator of 236, 239, 241, 245
   fictional confession 7, 241
   hearsay confession 226
   Helen's death by 6, 81–9, 94
   Madame de Pauw's death by 73–4
   Mrs Abercromby's death by 60
   no proof of TGW's use of 7, 128, 240
   stories attributed to TGW 105–6, 147, 228–31
   symptoms of 101–2
   tales inspired by TGW 6, 157, 224
   TGW's knowledge of 100–1
   TGW's letter concerning 173
Pollock, Sir Frederick (Attorney-general) 80, 131–8, 188, 236
Port Arthur 193
Porter, Hal 231
Power, Agnes 211
Power, Robert 202, 220

283

Pritchard, James 32
Proctor, B W *see* Cornwall, Barry
Provident insurance company 72–4, 91
Pym, Henrietta 243
Pym, William Wollaston 243, 247, 250

Red Barn murder 123–8
Richardson, Mary Lydia 244
Robinson, Mr 131
Robson, L L 181
*Rodney* 187
Royal Academy Summer Exhibition *44*
Royal Artillery Drivers 34–5
Rush, J L 188
*Rush v Peacock* 188
Ruskin, Effie 81
Ruskin, John 43, 46
Russell, Lord John 161, 167, 171, 174

6th Battalion Royal Artillery 35
16th (Bedfordshire) Regiment of Foot 21–9
Scott, John 41, 43–4
Seccombe, Thomas 59
Sharpus the moneylender 69, 76–7, 84, 86–7, 92, 139, 239
Sheriff of Middlesex 76
Siddons, Sarah 49
Slocombe, Francis 78
Smedley, William 111
Smith, Henry P 64, 91, 100, 113, 163, 165, 167, 169–74, 188, 225–6, 238, 241
Smollett, Tobias 9
Snell, Henry 115
Southey, Robert 18
strychnine 6, 36, 89, 94–102, 106, 132, 226, 230, 239, 241
Stuart, John 58
sudden deaths
    Frances Abercromby 5, 8, 33, 59–60, 240–1
    George Griffiths 5, 8, 56, 59, 240–1
    Helen Abercromby 5, 33–4, 76–93, 99

Sun Tzu 145
*Susan* 3–4, 174–5, 177–80, 183–7, 191, 221
Swinburne, Algernon Charles 43

Talfourd, Thomas 37–8, 47, 177
Tasman, Abel 191
Taylor, A J P 128
Taylor, Alfred Swaine 97, 99, 224
Ternan, Ellen 114
Thatcher, Margaret 128
*Theresa* 192
Thesiger, Mr 131
Thompson, Richard 100, 113–21, 158–9, 169, 226, 241
Thomson, James 221
Thornbury, Walter 38–9, 104–5, 163, 211, 229–30
Tomalin, Clare 114
transportation 4, 162, 164–6, 175–87, 193, 195, 208, 224, 231
Trebeck, A M 12
trials *see* court cases
Turner, J M W 39–40, 43, 46

Van Diemen, Antony 191
Van Diemen's Land 3–4, 179–82, 191–211, 221, 223, 231–2, 234, 241
Van Vinkbooms, Cornelius 42
Vaughan (Justice) 160, 163
Villard, Amelia Thomasina Symmes 146
Von Holst, Theodor 103, 146–9, 197

Wainewright, Ann (*née* Griffiths; TGW's mother) 12–14
Wainewright, Beatrice 244, 246–7
Wainewright, Claude Beauchamp 244, 246–9
Wainewright, Constance 244, 246–7
Wainewright, Edward 244, 246–7
Wainewright, Eliza Frances (née Ward; TGW's wife)
   accused by TGW 198, 206
   beneficiary of Helen's will 79, 87
   beneficiary of mother's will 59–60
   birth 34

birth of son 56–7
character modelled on 224–5
court cases 138–40, 188–90, 236–7
death 244–5
extravagant lifestyle 49–50, 242
financial difficulties 212–22, 241–2
forms of assignment 78
in genteel poverty 58, 108
as Helen's murderer? 84–5, 93, 133–4, 173, 236–41
as Helen's step-sister 35
insurance frauds 5, 62–75, 236, 238–41
marriage 36
name given as Fanny Cooper-Ward 248–9
possible nurse of TGW 33
separation from TGW 93, 147, 212–13
as witness to Madalina's marriage 108, 237
Wainewright, Griffiths (TGW's son)
  birth 56–7
  children 246–50
  death 247–9
  death of wife 247
  deprived of inheritance 169, 217
  early years 76, 84–5, 93, 108
  marriage 243
  military career 246–7
  mother's fears of workhouse for 213
  move to Canada 244
  relationship with mother 237, 243, 245
Wainewright, Lionel 250
Wainewright, Margaret 247
Wainewright, Robert (TGW's uncle) 15, 51, 79, 111–12, 149, 151
Wainewright, Thomas Griffiths
  army career 20–9
  arrest 106, 115–18, 120, 148–53, 158
  artistic career 4, 17–18, 20, 39–48, 54, 58, 151–2, 200–5, 234
  artistic works *19, 40, 68, 201, 203, 205, 207, 209*
  Bank of England fraud 5, 16, 36, 51–4, 62, 93, 110–12, 117–18, 122, 212, 240–1

birth 7, 12–13
confessions 6–7, 100, 169, 172–4, 198, 226
court cases 81, 97, 108, 113–14, 129–40, 152, 160–6, 188–90
dandyism 17–18, 37–9, 152
death 210–11, 220–2, 226
education 17
extravagant lifestyle 49–51, 242
in France 103–4, 106–10, 114–22, 135, 142, 158–9, 242
as guilty of murder? 236–42
insurance frauds 62–75, 90–3, 236, 238–41
involvement in Red Barn murder 123–8
knowledge of poison 100–1
Linden House
   deaths at 8, 56, 59–60, 80–94
   life at 57–61, 76–7, 84
   return to 8, 54–5
marriage 36
mental illness 30–3, 75, 241
in Newgate Prison 53, 153–60, 166, 175, 230
noms-de-plume 41–2, 103
offer of betrayal 142–8
petitions for clemency 56, 106–7, 146, 149, 167–75, 195, 197–8, 204, 206, 208, 228, 232–4
physical appearance 37–8, 104, 192, 227–9
as poisoner 6–7, 100–1, 105–6, 128, 147, 157, 173, 224, 228–31, 240
portrayals of character 223–31
relationship with grandfather 12–16
separation from wife 93, 147, 212–13
son's birth 56–7
testimonials 198–9, 202, 208, 228, 232–5, *233*
transportation 4, 164–6, 175–87, 193, 195
upbringing 13, 16
in Van Diemen's Land 3–4, 191–211, 221, 223, 231–2, 234, 241

Wainewright, Thomas (TGW's father) 12–14
*Wainewright v Bland* 130–1
Wainewright, Victor Charles 249–50

Wainewright, Winnifred 249–50
Wainewright, Wollaston Guy 250
Walker, James Backhouse 195
Ward, Cooper 33–4
Ward, John Cooper 34–5
Wellesley, Arthur *see* Duke of Wellington
Wells, H G 94
Wheatley, Benjamin 58, 69, 93, 103, 108, 140–1, 237
Wheatley, Leonard Abercromby 108
Whorton, J C 95
Wilde, Oscar 6, 27–8, 30, 147–8, 157, 230–1
Williams, Theodore G 103, 110, 114, 119
wills
   Frances Abercromby 59–60, 240
   George Griffiths 57
   Helen Abercromby 77–80, 87, 92–3, 106, 129–31, 139–40, 174, 188, 238
   Ralph Griffiths 13–16, 32, 51
Wilson, John 183, 185
Woodford, Jonas Rogers 151
Woodham-Smith, C 28
Wordsworth, William 30, 39, 41

*York* 166, 175–8, *182*
Young, Mr 108

www.ingramcontent.com/pod-product-compliance
Lightning Source LLC
Chambersburg PA
CBHW031945080426
42735CB00007B/269

# The Handbook of
# Palmistry

by

Ray Douglas

DREAMSTAIRWAY

*The Handbook of Palmistry* was first published in the UK in 1995 by Cassell plc under the title *Palmistry and the Inner Self*. This edition with amendments and additions was published in 2009 by Dreamstairway.

© Ray Douglas 1995 and 2009       www.dreamstairway.co.uk

ISBN 978-1-907091-00-1

British Library Cataloguing in Publication Data
A catalogue record for this book is available from the British Library